5 INGREDIENTS
AIR FRYER
COOKBOOK

1800 Days of Quick and Easy Recipes, Perfectly **Portioned for Two**.
Cheat Sheet Included.

Violet Harmond

TABLE OF CONTENT

IS CRISPY, IS TASTY
BUT IS NOT FRIED!

INTRODUCING YOUR CULINARY ADVENTURE

Congratulations on embarking on a flavorful journey through the world of air frying! In the pages that follow, you'll discover a collection of delectable, easy-to-follow recipes, each designed for two servings and created exclusively for your air fryer.

Whether you're a seasoned chef or just getting started in the kitchen, these recipes are tailored to bring out the best in your air fryer. You'll be amazed by the versatility and convenience it offers, making every dish a delightful culinary experience.

LEAVE A REVIEW AND GET MORE!

If you enjoy the recipes and find this book to be a valuable addition to your culinary library, we'd greatly appreciate your feedback. Your honest review on Amazon not only supports us but also helps other food enthusiasts discover the world of air fryer cooking. It's your chance to share your experience and insights, and we'd love to hear from you.

UNLOCK EXCLUSIVE BONUSES

As a token of our appreciation, we've prepared a set of exclusive bonuses to enhance your air frying experience. At the end of this book, you'll find a QR code that, when scanned, will grant you access to:
Bonus recipes to expand your air fryer repertoire.

- A downloadable meal planning guide to help you make the most of your air fryer in your daily cooking.
- Helpful tips and tricks to further master your air fryer.

Thank you for choosing our book as your guide to air fryer cooking. We hope you thoroughly enjoy every recipe, savor every bite, and create countless memorable meals for you and your loved ones.

Let's get started and experience the magic of air frying together!

THE AIR FRYER ADVANTAGE

In the age of kitchen innovation, the air fryer stands out as a remarkable and versatile appliance. It offers a transformative cooking experience that allows you to savor the crispy, golden goodness of your favorite dishes without the guilt of excessive oil.

The secret? Rapid air circulation that cooks your food to perfection while preserving its flavor and moisture. You can enjoy the delightful crunch of fried foods with just a fraction of the oil, making your meals healthier and more enjoyable.

WHY YOU NEED AN AIR FRYER

In this section, we'll delve deeper into the reasons why an air fryer is a valuable addition to your kitchen. Let's explore some specific examples that highlight the benefits of owning and using an air fryer:

Healthier Cooking Options: One of the primary reasons you need an air fryer is its ability to prepare healthier meals. Traditional deep frying involves submerging food in hot oil, which can add excessive calories and unhealthy fats to your dishes. With an air fryer, you can achieve the same crispy and delicious results using significantly less oil or even none at all. For example, imagine enjoying crispy, golden-brown chicken wings with just a fraction of the fat and calories of traditionally fried wings.

Reduced Fat and Calories: Air frying offers a substantial reduction in the fat content of your favorite dishes. Consider how you can relish homemade french fries with up to 70-80% less oil, leading to a healthier and guilt-free snacking option. The hot air circulation in the air fryer cooks the food to perfection while excess fat drips away into a separate tray.

Time and Energy Savings: Your air fryer is a time-saving kitchen companion. It preheats quickly, and the efficient cooking process often results in faster meal preparation. For example, you can enjoy a perfectly cooked salmon fillet in under 10 minutes, sparing you valuable time on busy weeknights. Additionally, because air fryers are smaller and more energy-efficient than traditional ovens, they consume less electricity, helping you save on your energy bills.

Versatile Cooking: An air fryer is incredibly versatile. It's not just for frying; you can bake, roast, grill, and even dehydrate food in this compact appliance. Imagine being able to make a batch of perfectly crispy and flavorful sweet potato fries one day and a tender, juicy roast chicken the next. The air fryer's versatility opens up a world of culinary possibilities.

Minimal Odor and Mess: Traditional deep frying can leave your kitchen with a lingering, unpleasant odor. With an air fryer, there's minimal to no odor, thanks to the enclosed cooking chamber and the absence of large quantities of hot oil. Additionally, cleaning up after air frying is a breeze. For example, you can cook a batch of homemade mozzarella sticks with ease and quickly wipe down the air fryer, leaving your kitchen smelling fresh and clean.

Dietary Accommodations: An air fryer is an excellent tool for accommodating various dietary preferences and restrictions. Whether you're cooking for someone on a low-fat diet, following a specific eating plan like keto, or catering to a vegan lifestyle, the air fryer's adaptability makes it easy to prepare meals that meet specific dietary needs. You can effortlessly create gluten-free dishes, vegetable-forward options, and much more.

These examples showcase the compelling reasons why an air fryer is a must-have kitchen appliance. From healthier cooking and time savings to versatility and ease of use, your air fryer will revolutionize your culinary experience and provide endless opportunities for creating delicious, guilt-free meals.

GETTING TO KNOW YOUR AIR FRYER

Understanding the Different Components: Your air fryer is a versatile kitchen appliance with various components. These typically include the cooking basket, the fryer drawer, a control panel, and a heating element. For instance, in a popular air fryer model, such as the Philips Airfryer, the cooking basket has a mesh bottom to allow hot air to circulate around the food. The fryer drawer houses the basket and is where you place your ingredients. The control panel consists of temperature and time settings, allowing you to customize your cooking. Understanding these components is crucial for effective and safe operation.

Selecting the Right Air Fryer for You: When purchasing an air fryer, consider factors like the cooking capacity, available presets, and additional features. For example, the COSORI Air Fryer offers various sizes, allowing you to choose the one that best suits your needs, whether you're cooking for one or a family. Some models come with presets for specific dishes, such as chicken, fries, or fish, which can simplify cooking. Also, some air fryers include features like a shake reminder, which prompts you to shake the basket during cooking for even results. Evaluating these aspects will help you find the perfect air fryer for your kitchen.

Digital vs. Manual Controls: Air fryers come with either digital or manual controls. The Ninja Foodi, for instance, features digital controls that offer precise temperature and time settings with the push of a button. In contrast, the Instant Vortex has manual dials for adjusting the settings. The choice between digital and manual controls depends on your preference. Digital controls provide accuracy and often offer presets for various recipes, while manual dials give you a more tactile and hands-on experience. Understanding your air fryer's control system is essential for successful cooking.

Tips for Efficient Usage: To maximize the efficiency of your air fryer, it's crucial to preheat it as needed. For example, the GoWISE USA Air Fryer typically requires a short preheating time to ensure that the cooking chamber is at the desired temperature before adding your ingredients. Additionally, be mindful of the cooking time and temperature settings for different recipes. Air fryers cook food faster than conventional methods, so keep an eye on your dishes to prevent overcooking. Familiarizing yourself with these usage tips will help you become a proficient air fryer chef.

Safety Precautions: Safety should always be a top priority when using your air fryer. For example, the Cuisinart AirFryer Toaster Oven features an auto-shutoff function when the door is opened, ensuring safety during operation. It's essential to place your air fryer on a stable, heat-resistant surface, away from flammable materials. Additionally, avoid overcrowding the cooking basket to allow proper air circulation, which ensures even cooking. Knowing and adhering to these safety precautions will help you enjoy your air fryer worry-free.

Exploring Accessories: Many air fryers come with additional accessories like baking pans, racks, and skewers. For example, the Breville Smart Oven Air includes a variety of accessories that expand your cooking options. These accessories can be used to prepare a wide range of dishes, from roasting a whole chicken to baking a cake. Understanding how to use these accessories effectively can open up a world of possibilities in air frying.

By getting to know the different components, selecting the right air fryer, understanding control systems, following usage tips, prioritizing safety, and exploring available accessories, you'll be well-equipped to make the most of your air fryer. This knowledge forms the foundation for successful air frying and sets the stage for your culinary journey.

USING YOUR AIR FRYER SAFELY

Using an air fryer is a relatively straightforward process, but it's crucial to prioritize safety and follow some essential guidelines. Here, we'll delve into how to use your air fryer safely and provide examples to illustrate these safety measures:

Positioning Your Air Fryer:

- Place your air fryer on a flat, heat-resistant surface with adequate clearance around it.
- Keep it away from walls, curtains, and other flammable materials.
- Ensure proper ventilation by leaving sufficient space on all sides for air circulation.

Preheating and Monitoring:

- Preheat your air fryer as needed, following recipe instructions. This ensures even cooking.
- Monitor the cooking process regularly to prevent overcooking or burning. Example:

When making air-fried chicken, preheat the air fryer and check the chicken's internal temperature to ensure it's thoroughly cooked.

Basket Loading:

- Arrange food items in a single layer in the air fryer basket.
- Avoid overcrowding, which can hinder air circulation and result in uneven cooking. Example: When making French fries, spread them out evenly to achieve crispy results.

Hot Surfaces:

- Be cautious of hot surfaces, including the basket, tray, and interior components.
- Use oven mitts or tongs when removing items from the air fryer to prevent burns. Example: When preparing cinnamon sugar donut holes, use tongs to safely remove the hot, crispy donuts from the air fryer.

Grease Management:

- Empty the grease tray or drawer after each use to prevent the accumulation of excess grease.
- Dispose of grease properly and avoid pouring it down the sink to prevent clogs. Example: When cooking bacon-wrapped asparagus, be sure to empty the grease tray and dispose of the bacon grease responsibly.

Children and Pets:

- Keep children and pets at a safe distance when the air fryer is in use.
- Ensure that the air fryer is placed out of their reach to prevent accidents. Example: When making air-fried apple pie egg rolls, create a safe cooking environment by keeping curious children and pets away from the hot appliance.

Proper Cord Management:

- Keep the power cord away from hot surfaces and sharp edges.
- Avoid letting the cord dangle or be exposed to excessive heat. Example: When air frying churro bites, make sure the power cord is neatly arranged and does not interfere with the air fryer's operation.

Ventilation and Smoke:

- Ensure proper ventilation by keeping the air intake and exhaust vents clear.
- Be prepared for some smoke when cooking high-fat items, and use your air fryer in a well-ventilated area. Example: When making crispy air-fried bacon, open a window or use a range hood to manage smoke and odors.

These safety measures and examples are essential for a smooth and secure air frying experience. By following these guidelines, you can use your air fryer with confidence and enjoy delicious, crispy results while ensuring the safety of your kitchen and family.

RECIPE ADAPTATIONS FOR AIR FRYING

One of the great things about owning an air fryer is its versatility in preparing a wide range of dishes. While many recipes can be made directly in the air fryer, you can also adapt your favorite traditional recipes to take advantage of air frying's benefits. Here are some key points and examples:

REDUCING OIL AND FAT

One of the primary advantages of air frying is the ability to enjoy the crispy, fried texture without excessive oil. You can adapt recipes that are traditionally deep-fried by using minimal oil or even none at all. For instance:

- **Traditional Recipe:** Deep-Fried Chicken Wings
- **Air Fryer Adaptation:** Instead of deep frying, lightly coat the wings with a small amount of oil and air fry them to crispy perfection. The hot air circulation will give them a similar crispy texture.

ADJUSTING COOKING TIMES AND TEMPERATURES

Air fryers typically cook faster than conventional ovens, so adjusting the cooking time and temperature is crucial. Here's an example:

- **Traditional Recipe:** Baked Sweet Potato Fries
- **Air Fryer Adaptation:** Reduce the temperature and cooking time from what the oven recipe recommends. This results in crispy sweet potato fries in a fraction of the time.

USING AIR FRYER ACCESSORIES

Air fryers often come with accessories like grill racks, skewers, and baking pans. These can expand your cooking possibilities. For instance:

- **Traditional Recipe:** Oven-Roasted Vegetables
- **Air Fryer Adaptation:** Use the air fryer's grill rack to cook vegetables with a perfect sear and texture, similar to grilling but without the need for an outdoor grill.

MAKING HEALTHIER SNACKS

Transform your favorite snack recipes into healthier versions by air frying. This is especially useful for snacks that are typically fried or greasy. For example:

- **Traditional Recipe:** Potato Chips
- **Air Fryer Adaptation:** Slice potatoes thinly, lightly spray them with oil, season with your favorite spices, and air fry them to create crispy, guilt-free potato chips.

CONVERTING CONVENTIONAL RECIPES

If you have an oven-baked or pan-fried recipe, you can often convert it into an air fryer recipe with ease. Consider:

- **Traditional Recipe:** Oven-Baked Salmon
- **Air Fryer Adaptation:** Marinate your salmon, place it in the air fryer basket, and cook at a slightly lower temperature for a shorter time. The result is tender, flaky salmon with a perfectly crispy exterior.

EXPERIMENTING WITH DIFFERENT CUISINES

Don't limit yourself to classic air fryer recipes. Try adapting dishes from various cuisines to the air fryer. For instance:

- **Traditional Recipe:** Tempura Shrimp
- **Air Fryer Adaptation:** Use a light tempura batter on shrimp, then air fry them for a healthier and equally delicious version of this Japanese favorite.

By understanding these adaptation techniques, you can take full advantage of your air fryer's capabilities and enjoy healthier, crispy, and delicious versions of your favorite meals and snacks. Experiment, adjust, and discover new ways to make your dishes shine in the air fryer.

MAINTAINING YOUR AIR FRYER

Proper maintenance of your air fryer is crucial for ensuring its longevity and performance. Regular care and cleaning will help you continue to enjoy delicious, healthy meals with your air fryer. Here are some key maintenance tips and examples:

REGULAR CLEANING:

- After each use, allow your air fryer to cool down.
- Wipe down the interior and exterior with a damp cloth to remove any food residue or grease.
- Clean the basket and tray with warm, soapy water, or place them in the dishwasher if they are dishwasher-safe.
- Check the heating element and fan for any debris and clean if necessary.

CLEANING THE HEATING ELEMENT:

- Over time, the heating element may accumulate grease and food particles, affecting its efficiency.
- Use a soft brush or cloth to gently wipe away any buildup from the heating element.
- Be sure not to damage the element during cleaning, and always do this when the air fryer is cool and unplugged.

DEALING WITH TOUGH STAINS:

- For stubborn stains or baked-on residue, create a paste using baking soda and water.
- Apply the paste to the affected area, let it sit for a few minutes, and then scrub gently with a soft brush or cloth.
- Rinse thoroughly to remove the paste.

PREVENTING ODOR BUILDUP:

- If your air fryer starts to develop odors, place a small bowl of water with lemon slices or vinegar in the cooking chamber.
- Run the air fryer at a low temperature for a few minutes to help remove the odors.

CHECKING THE SEALS:

- Periodically inspect the seals and gaskets to ensure they are not damaged or loose.

- Damaged seals can affect the efficiency of your air fryer and may need to be replaced.

DESCALING THE HEATING ELEMENT:

- In hard water areas, mineral deposits can accumulate on the heating element.
- To descale, mix equal parts of water and vinegar in the cooking chamber and run the air fryer for a short cycle.
- Follow this with a cycle of plain water to rinse out any remaining vinegar.

REPLACING WORN PARTS:

- As your air fryer ages, some components may wear out or become less effective.
- Keep an eye on the condition of the basket, tray, and any removable parts. If they show signs of wear, consider replacing them to maintain optimal performance.

STORING YOUR AIR FRYER:

- When not in use, store your air fryer in a dry and cool place.
- Avoid storing it with the basket and tray inside to prevent any odors or damage.
- Ensure the air fryer is completely dry before storing to prevent mold or mildew growth.

Proper maintenance not only extends the life of your air fryer but also ensures that it continues to function at its best, producing delicious meals. Regular cleaning and care will make air frying a breeze and help you enjoy its benefits for years to come.

CLEANING YOUR AIR FRYER

Cleaning your air fryer is a crucial part of its maintenance, ensuring it continues to perform at its best and that your cooked meals taste as delicious as ever. Here's a detailed guide on how to clean your air fryer, complete with practical examples:

STEP 1: Unplug and Cool Down

Before you begin cleaning your air fryer, make sure it's unplugged and fully cooled down. This will prevent any accidental burns and ensure your safety.

STEP 2: Disassemble the Air Fryer

Start by disassembling the removable parts of your air fryer. This typically includes the cooking basket or tray, the pan, and any other detachable components. *Here's an example using a popular model:*
If you own a Phillips Airfryer, remove the cooking basket by pushing the release button and sliding it out. Take out the pan and any other removable parts as per your model's design.

STEP 3: Wash the Removable Parts

The removable parts are usually dishwasher-safe, but hand washing is often recommended to prolong their lifespan. Use warm, soapy water to clean them thoroughly. Here's an example:
Wash the cooking basket and pan with warm, soapy water and a soft sponge or cloth. Make sure to remove any food residue or grease. If there are stubborn stains, let them soak for a few minutes before scrubbing gently.

STEP 4: Clean the Interior and Exterior

The interior of the air fryer can accumulate grease and food particles during cooking. Wipe it clean with a damp cloth or sponge. Pay special attention to the heating element. Avoid using abrasive materials that might scratch the non-stick surface. For the exterior, simply wipe it down with a damp cloth. *Examples include:*
Gently wipe the interior of the air fryer to remove any residue. Be cautious around the heating

element. For the exterior, wipe off any spills or stains to keep the exterior looking clean and presentable.

STEP 5: Dealing with Stubborn Stains

If there are tough, baked-on stains, you can use a mixture of baking soda and water to create a paste. Apply the paste to the stains, let it sit for a while, and then scrub it off. *An example:*
For stubborn, stuck-on food, create a paste by mixing baking soda and water. Apply this paste to the stains and let it sit for 10-15 minutes. Afterward, gently scrub with a non-abrasive sponge or cloth.

STEP 6: Reassemble the Air Fryer

After cleaning and ensuring everything is dry, reassemble your air fryer. Make sure all parts are securely in place and ready for the next use.
Example: Reinsert the pan and cooking basket into your air fryer, ensuring they fit securely. Check that all components are properly assembled.

By following these cleaning steps, you'll keep your air fryer in great condition and ensure it remains a reliable kitchen companion. It's important to consult your specific air fryer's user manual for model-specific cleaning instructions and safety recommendations.

BREAKFAST

1. AIR FRIED BREAKFAST BURRITOS

 Prep time: 10 minutes   **Servings:** 2

INGREDIENTS:

- 4 large eggs
- 1/2 cup diced bell peppers
- 1/4 cup shredded cheddar cheese
- 2 large flour tortillas

NUTRITIONAL INFO (PER SERVING):

Cal: 345 | Carbs: 29g | Pro: 16g
Fat: 18g | Sugars: 3g | Fiber: 2g

INSTRUCTIONS:

1. Preheat the air fryer to 350°F (180°C).
2. In a bowl, beat the eggs and stir in the diced bell peppers.
3. Pour the egg mixture into the air fryer basket and cook for 5 minutes, stirring occasionally.
4. Place the tortillas in the air fryer for 1-2 minutes to warm them.
5. Divide the scrambled eggs and shredded cheese evenly between the two tortillas.
6. Fold the tortillas to form burritos.
7. Place the burritos in the air fryer and cook for an additional 2-3 minutes until they're crispy and golden.
8. Serve and enjoy!

2. AIR FRYER FRENCH TOAST STICKS

 Prep time: 5 minutes   **Servings:** 2

INGREDIENTS:

- 4 slices of bread
- 2 eggs
- 1/4 cup milk
- 1/2 teaspoon cinnamon

NUTRITIONAL INFO (PER SERVING):

Cal: 213 | Carbs: 31g | Pro: 11g
Fat: 6g | Sugars: 6g | Fiber: 2g

INSTRUCTIONS:

1. Preheat the air fryer to 350°F (180°C).
2. Cut each slice of bread into three sticks.
3. In a shallow bowl, whisk together the eggs, milk, and cinnamon.
4. Dip the bread sticks into the egg mixture, making sure they're well-coated.
5. Place the coated sticks in the air fryer basket.
6. Air fry for 5-6 minutes, turning them halfway through, until they are golden and crispy.
7. Serve with maple syrup or your favorite dipping sauce.

3. BREAKFAST QUESADILLAS

 Prep time: 15 minutes   **Servings:** 2

INGREDIENTS:

- 4 small flour tortillas
- 4 large eggs
- 1/2 cup shredded cheddar cheese
- 1/4 cup diced ham

NUTRITIONAL INFO (PER SERVING):

Cal: 439 | Carbs: 26g | Pro: 26g
Fat: 25g | Sugars: 1g | Fiber: 2g

INSTRUCTIONS:

1. Preheat the air fryer to 350°F (180°C).
2. Scramble the eggs in a bowl.
3. Place two tortillas on a clean surface.
4. Sprinkle half of the shredded cheddar cheese evenly on each tortilla.
5. Add half of the diced ham on top of the cheese.
6. Pour half of the scrambled eggs over the ham and cheese.
7. Place the remaining tortillas on top to form quesadillas.
8. Air fry for 5-7 minutes until they're crispy and the cheese is melted.
9. Let them cool for a minute, then cut into wedges and serve.

4. AIR FRIED AVOCADO TOAST

 Prep time: 5 minutes   **Servings:** 2

INGREDIENTS:

- 1 ripe avocado
- 2 slices of whole-grain bread
- 1/2 teaspoon red pepper flakes (optional)
- Salt and pepper to taste

NUTRITIONAL INFO (PER SERVING):

Cal: 231 | Carbs: 16g | Pro: 4g
Fat: 18g | Sugars: 1g | Fiber: 8g

INSTRUCTIONS:

1. Cut the avocado in half, remove the pit, and scoop the flesh into a bowl. Mash it with a fork.
2. Season the mashed avocado with red pepper flakes, salt, and pepper.
3. Toast the bread slices until they're crispy in the air fryer for 2-3 minutes.
4. Spread the seasoned avocado evenly on the toasted bread.
5. Serve immediately.

5. BACON AND EGG MUFFINS

 Prep time: 15 minutes   **Servings:** 2

INGREDIENTS:

- 2 English muffins, split
- 4 large eggs
- 2 slices of bacon
- Salt and pepper to taste

NUTRITIONAL INFO (PER SERVING):

Cal: 287 | Carbs: 26g | Pro: 15g
Fat: 14g | Sugars: 2g | Fiber: 2g

INSTRUCTIONS:

1. Preheat the air fryer to 350°F (180°C).
2. Place the English muffin halves in the air fryer and toast for 2-3 minutes until they're crispy.
3. While the muffins are toasting, place the bacon slices in the air fryer and cook for 5-7 minutes until they're crispy.
4. Remove the bacon and English muffins from the air fryer.
5. Crack the eggs into a bowl, season with salt and pepper, and whisk.
6. Pour the beaten eggs into the air fryer and cook for 5-6 minutes until they're set.
7. Assemble the muffins with bacon, eggs, and the top halves of the English muffins.
8. Serve hot.

6. CINNAMON SUGAR DONUT HOLES

 Prep time: 10 minutes   **Servings:** 2

INGREDIENTS:

- 1 can of refrigerated biscuit dough
- 2 tablespoons melted butter
- 1/4 cup granulated sugar
- 1 teaspoon ground cinnamon

NUTRITIONAL INFO (PER SERVING):

Cal: 284 | Carbs: 35g | Pro: 2g
Fat: 15g | Sugars: 13g | Fiber: 1g

INSTRUCTIONS:

1. Preheat the air fryer to 350°F (180°C).
2. Open the can of biscuit dough and separate it into individual biscuits.
3. Roll each biscuit into a small ball to create donut holes.
4. Brush the donut holes with melted butter.
5. In a bowl, combine sugar and cinnamon.
6. Roll the buttered donut holes in the cinnamon sugar mixture.
7. Place the donut holes in the air fryer and cook for 6-8 minutes until they're golden brown and cooked through.
8. Serve warm.

7. AIR FRYER OMELETTE

 Prep time: 10 minutes   **Servings:** 2

INGREDIENTS:

- 4 large eggs
- 1/2 cup diced bell peppers
- 1/4 cup diced onions
- 1/4 cup shredded cheddar cheese

NUTRITIONAL INFO (PER SERVING):

Cal: 276 | Carbs: 6g | Pro: 17g
Fat: 20g | Sugars: 3g | Fiber: 1g

INSTRUCTIONS:

1. Preheat the air fryer to 350°F (180°C).
2. In a bowl, beat the eggs and stir in the diced bell peppers and onions.
3. Pour the egg mixture into the air fryer basket.
4. Cook for 5-6 minutes, stirring occasionally until the eggs are almost set.
5. Sprinkle the shredded cheddar cheese on top.
6. Continue cooking for 2-3 minutes until the cheese is melted, and the omelette is fully cooked.
7. Carefully remove the omelette from the air fryer and fold it in half.
8. Serve hot.

8. AIR FRIED BREAKFAST POTATOES

 Prep time: 10 minutes   **Servings:** 2

INGREDIENTS:

- 2 medium potatoes, diced
- 2 tablespoons olive oil
- 1/2 teaspoon paprika
- Salt and pepper to taste

NUTRITIONAL INFO (PER SERVING):

Cal: 233 | Carbs: 28g | Pro: 3g
Fat: 12g | Sugars: 1g | Fiber: 4g

INSTRUCTIONS:

1. Preheat the air fryer to 400°F (200°C).
2. In a bowl, toss the diced potatoes with olive oil, paprika, salt, and pepper.
3. Place the seasoned potatoes in the air fryer basket.
4. Air fry for 15-20 minutes, shaking the basket every 5 minutes until the potatoes are crispy and golden.
5. Serve as a side with your favorite breakfast items.

9. BANANA NUT MUFFINS

 Prep time: 15 minutes   **Servings:** 2

INGREDIENTS:

- 1 ripe banana, mashed
- 1/2 cup self-rising flour
- 1/4 cup chopped nuts (e.g., walnuts or pecans)
- 2 tablespoons honey

NUTRITIONAL INFO (PER SERVING):

Cal: 315 | Carbs: 63g | Pro: 7g
Fat: 7g | Sugars: 25g | Fiber: 4g

INSTRUCTIONS:

1. Preheat the air fryer to 325°F (160°C).
2. In a bowl, combine the mashed banana, self-rising flour, chopped nuts, and honey.
3. Mix until well combined.
4. Divide the batter into two greased ramekins.
5. Place the ramekins in the air fryer and air fry for 12-15 minutes until the muffins are firm and a toothpick comes out clean.
6. Allow to cool slightly before serving.

10. SAUSAGE AND CHEESE BREAKFAST BISCUITS

 Prep time: 10 minutes   **Servings:** 2

INGREDIENTS:

- 2 frozen biscuit dough rounds
- 2 cooked breakfast sausages
- 1/4 cup shredded cheddar cheese

NUTRITIONAL INFO (PER SERVING):

Cal: 407 | Carbs: 30g | Pro: 14g
Fat: 26g | Sugars: 4g | Fiber: 1g

INSTRUCTIONS:

1. Preheat the air fryer to 350°F (180°C).
2. Place the frozen biscuit dough rounds in the air fryer and cook for 5-7 minutes until they're golden.
3. While the biscuits are cooking, slice the cooked sausages in half.
4. When the biscuits are done, split them in half.
5. Place a sausage patty and shredded cheddar cheese on the bottom half of each biscuit.
6. Place the top half back on and return them to the air fryer for 2-3 minutes to melt the cheese.
7. Serve hot.

11. BLUEBERRY PANCAKE BITES

 Prep time: 15 minutes   **Servings:** 2

INGREDIENTS:

- 1/2 cup pancake mix
- 1/4 cup milk
- 1/4 cup blueberries
- 1/2 tablespoon butter

NUTRITIONAL INFO (PER SERVING):

Cal: 226 | Carbs: 34g | Pro: 6g
Fat: 7g | Sugars: 6g | Fiber: 1g

INSTRUCTIONS:

1. Preheat the air fryer to 350°F (180°C).
2. In a bowl, mix the pancake mix and milk until smooth.
3. Gently fold in the blueberries.
4. Grease a silicone muffin mold with the butter.
5. Pour the pancake batter into the muffin cups.
6. Air fry for 8-10 minutes until they're golden and set.
7. Serve with maple syrup.

12. BREAKFAST SAUSAGE LINKS

 Prep time: 5 minutes   **Servings:** 2

INGREDIENTS:

- 8 breakfast sausage links
- Cooking spray

NUTRITIONAL INFO (PER SERVING):

Cal: 252 | Carbs: 1g | Pro: 10g
Fat: 23g | Sugars: 0g | Fiber: 0g

INSTRUCTIONS:

1. Preheat the air fryer to 350°F (180°C).
2. Spray the air fryer basket with cooking spray to prevent sticking.
3. Place the breakfast sausage links in the air fryer.
4. Air fry for 8-10 minutes, turning them halfway through, until they're browned and cooked through.
5. Serve with your choice of breakfast sides.

13. AIR FRYER BREAKFAST PIZZA

 Prep time: 10 minutes   **Servings:** 2

INGREDIENTS:

- 2 small pizza crusts
- 1/4 cup pizza sauce
- 1/2 cup shredded mozzarella cheese
- 2 large eggs

NUTRITIONAL INFO (PER SERVING):

Cal: 414 | Carbs: 34g | Pro: 23g
Fat: 19g | Sugars: 3g | Fiber: 2g

INSTRUCTIONS:

1. Preheat the air fryer to 350°F (180°C).
2. Spread pizza sauce evenly on each pizza crust.
3. Sprinkle shredded mozzarella cheese on top.
4. Create a well in the center of each pizza.
5. Carefully crack an egg into the well of each pizza.
6. Place the pizzas in the air fryer and cook for 8-10 minutes, or until the egg whites are set.
7. Serve hot.

14. BREAKFAST TAQUITOS

 Prep time: 15 minutes   **Servings:** 2

INGREDIENTS:

- 4 small flour tortillas
- 2 large eggs, scrambled
- 1/2 cup diced ham
- 1/4 cup shredded cheddar cheese

NUTRITIONAL INFO (PER SERVING):

Cal: 394 | Carbs: 26g | Pro: 20g
Fat: 24g | Sugars: 1g | Fiber: 2g

INSTRUCTIONS:

1. Preheat the air fryer to 350°F (180°C).
2. Warm the tortillas in the air fryer for 1-2 minutes.
3. In a bowl, scramble the eggs.
4. Divide the scrambled eggs, diced ham, and shredded cheddar cheese evenly between the tortillas.
5. Roll up the tortillas to form taquitos.
6. Place the taquitos in the air fryer and cook for 4-5 minutes until they're crispy and heated through.
7. Serve with salsa or your favorite dipping sauce.

15. CHEESY HASH BROWNS

 Prep time: 10 minutes   **Servings:** 2

INGREDIENTS:

- 2 cups frozen hash browns
- 1/2 cup shredded cheddar cheese
- 1/4 teaspoon garlic powder
- Salt and pepper to taste

NUTRITIONAL INFO (PER SERVING):

Cal: 255 | Carbs: 22g | Pro: 9g
Fat: 15g | Sugars: 0g | Fiber: 2g

INSTRUCTIONS:

1. Preheat the air fryer to 375°F (190°C).
2. In a bowl, mix the frozen hash browns, shredded cheddar cheese, garlic powder, salt, and pepper.
3. Place the hash brown mixture in the air fryer basket.
4. Air fry for 12-15 minutes, shaking the basket every 5 minutes, until the hash browns are crispy and golden.
5. Serve as a delicious side for your breakfast.

16. SPINACH AND FETA BREAKFAST WRAPS

 Prep time: 10 minutes   **Servings:** 2

INGREDIENTS:

- 2 large flour tortillas
- 2 cups fresh spinach
- 1/4 cup crumbled feta cheese
- 2 large eggs

NUTRITIONAL INFO (PER SERVING):

Cal: 297 | Carbs: 25g | Pro: 13g
Fat: 17g | Sugars: 1g | Fiber: 2g

INSTRUCTIONS:

1. Preheat the air fryer to 350°F (180°C).
2. In a bowl, beat the eggs.
3. Spray the air fryer basket with cooking spray.
4. Place the spinach in the basket and pour the beaten eggs over it.
5. Air fry for 5-6 minutes, stirring occasionally, until the eggs are set.
6. Warm the tortillas in the air fryer for 1-2 minutes.
7. Divide the scrambled eggs, spinach, and crumbled feta cheese between the tortillas.
8. Roll up the tortillas to form wraps.
9. Serve immediately.

17. APPLE CINNAMON OATMEAL

 Prep time: 10 minutes   **Servings:** 2

INGREDIENTS:

- 1 cup rolled oats
- 2 cups water
- 1 apple, peeled, cored, and diced
- 1/2 teaspoon ground cinnamon

NUTRITIONAL INFO (PER SERVING):

Cal: 222 | Carbs: 47g | Pro: 6g
Fat: 2g | Sugars: 12g | Fiber: 6g

INSTRUCTIONS:

1. Preheat the air fryer to 350°F (180°C).
2. In an oven-safe dish that fits in the air fryer, combine rolled oats, water, diced apple, and ground cinnamon.
3. Place the dish in the air fryer.
4. Air fry for 15-20 minutes, stirring occasionally, until the oats are cooked and the apples are tender.
5. Serve hot with a drizzle of honey or a sprinkle of extra cinnamon if desired.

18. VEGGIE BREAKFAST TACOS

 Prep time: 15 minutes   **Servings:** 2

INGREDIENTS:

- 4 small corn tortillas
- 2 large eggs
- 1/2 cup diced bell peppers
- 1/4 cup diced onions

NUTRITIONAL INFO (PER SERVING):

Cal: 192 | Carbs: 28g | Pro: 8g
Fat: 5g | Sugars: 2g | Fiber: 4g

INSTRUCTIONS:

1. Preheat the air fryer to 350°F (180°C).
2. Place the corn tortillas in the air fryer for 2-3 minutes to warm them.
3. In a bowl, beat the eggs.
4. Spray the air fryer basket with cooking spray.
5. Pour the beaten eggs, diced bell peppers, and diced onions into the basket.
6. Air fry for 5-6 minutes, stirring occasionally until the eggs are scrambled and vegetables are tender.
7. Divide the scrambled eggs and veggies between the tortillas.
8. Serve with your choice of salsa or hot sauce.

19. BREAKFAST SAUSAGE PATTIES

 Prep time: 10 minutes   **Servings:** 2

INGREDIENTS:

- 4 breakfast sausage patties
- Cooking spray

NUTRITIONAL INFO (PER SERVING):

Cal: 339 | Carbs: 0g | Pro: 11g
Fat: 32g | Sugars: 0g | Fiber: 0g

INSTRUCTIONS:

1. Preheat the air fryer to 350°F (180°C).
2. Spray the air fryer basket with cooking spray to prevent sticking.
3. Place the breakfast sausage patties in the air fryer.
4. Air fry for 8-10 minutes, turning them halfway through, until they're browned and cooked through.
5. Serve with your choice of breakfast sides.

20. CRANBERRY ORANGE SCONES

 Prep time: 15 minutes   **Servings:** 2

INGREDIENTS:

- 1 cup self-rising flour
- 2 tablespoons dried cranberries
- 1/2 teaspoon orange zest
- 1/4 cup milk

NUTRITIONAL INFO (PER SERVING):

Cal: 267 | Carbs: 59g | Pro: 6g
Fat: 1g | Sugars: 12g | Fiber: 2g

INSTRUCTIONS:

1. Preheat the air fryer to 325°F (160°C).
2. In a bowl, combine the self-rising flour, dried cranberries, and orange zest.
3. Add the milk and mix until a dough forms.
4. Divide the dough into two portions and shape them into scones.
5. Place the scones in the air fryer and air fry for 10-12 minutes until they're golden and cooked through.
6. Let them cool slightly before serving.

FIRST DISHES

1. AIR FRIED MOZZARELLA STICKS

 Prep time: 10 minutes   **Servings:** 2

INGREDIENTS:

- 8 mozzarella sticks
- 1 cup breadcrumbs
- 1 egg, beaten
- Cooking spray
- Marinara sauce for dipping

NUTRITIONAL INFO (PER SERVING):

Cal: 250 | Carbs: 20g | Pro: 15g
Fat: 12g | Sugars: 2g | Fiber: 2g

INSTRUCTIONS:

1. Preheat your air fryer to 375°F (190°C).
2. Cut each mozzarella stick in half to create 16 pieces.
3. Dip each mozzarella stick in beaten egg, then coat with breadcrumbs.
4. Place the coated mozzarella sticks in a single layer in the air fryer basket.
5. Lightly spray the sticks with cooking spray to help them crisp up.
6. Air fry for 5-7 minutes or until they are golden brown and crispy.
7. Serve immediately with marinara sauce for dipping.

2. SWEET POTATO FRIES WITH DIPPING SAUCE

 Prep time: 15 minutes   **Servings:** 2

INGREDIENTS:

- 2 medium sweet potatoes, cut into fries
- 2 tablespoons olive oil
- 1 teaspoon paprika
- Salt and pepper to taste
- 1/4 cup mayonnaise

NUTRITIONAL INFO (PER SERVING):

Cal: 320 | Carbs: 32g | Pro: 2g
Fat: 21g | Sugars: 6g | Fiber: 5g

INSTRUCTIONS:

1. In a bowl, toss sweet potato fries with olive oil, paprika, salt, and pepper.
2. Preheat your air fryer to 375°F (190°C).
3. Place the sweet potato fries in a single layer in the air fryer basket.
4. Air fry for 15-20 minutes, shaking the basket every 5 minutes for even cooking.
5. In the meantime, mix mayonnaise with a dash of paprika for the dipping sauce.
6. Serve the sweet potato fries hot with the dipping sauce.

3. ZUCCHINI PARMESAN CHIPS

 Prep time: 10 minutes   **Servings:** 2

INGREDIENTS:

- 2 medium zucchinis, sliced into rounds
- 1/2 cup grated Parmesan
- 1 teaspoon Italian seasoning
- Cooking spray
- Marinara sauce for dipping

NUTRITIONAL INFO (PER SERVING):

Cal: 120 | Carbs: 8g | Pro: 10g
Fat: 6g | Sugars: 4g | Fiber: 2g

INSTRUCTIONS:

1. Preheat your air fryer to 375°F (190°C).
2. In a bowl, mix the Parmesan cheese and Italian seasoning.
3. Dip each zucchini slice in the cheese mixture, coating both sides.
4. Place the coated zucchini slices in a single layer in the air fryer basket.
5. Lightly spray the slices with cooking spray.
6. Air fry for 7-10 minutes or until they are crispy and golden.
7. Serve with marinara sauce for dipping.

4. CRISPY EGGPLANT FRIES

 Prep time: 15 minutes   **Servings:** 2

INGREDIENTS:

- 1 small eggplant, cut into fries
- 1 cup breadcrumbs
- 1 egg, beaten
- Cooking spray
- Marinara sauce for dipping

NUTRITIONAL INFO (PER SERVING):

Cal: 220 | Carbs: 31g | Pro: 10g
Fat: 6g | Sugars: 4g | Fiber: 6g

INSTRUCTIONS:

1. Preheat your air fryer to 375°F (190°C).
2. Dip each eggplant fry in beaten egg, then coat with breadcrumbs.
3. Place the coated eggplant fries in a single layer in the air fryer basket.
4. Lightly spray the fries with cooking spray.
5. Air fry for 12-15 minutes or until they are golden and crispy.
6. Serve with marinara sauce for dipping.

5. GARLIC BREADSTICKS

 Prep time: 10 minutes   **Servings:** 2

INGREDIENTS:

- 4 pre-made breadsticks
- 2 tablespoons melted butter
- 2 cloves garlic, minced
- 1 tablespoon chopped fresh parsley
- Grated Parmesan cheese

NUTRITIONAL INFO (PER SERVING):

Cal: 230 | Carbs: 26g | Pro: 4g
Fat: 13g | Sugars: 2g | Fiber: 1g

INSTRUCTIONS:

1. Preheat your air fryer to 350°F (175°C).
2. In a small bowl, mix the melted butter, minced garlic, and chopped parsley.
3. Brush the garlic butter mixture over the breadsticks.
4. Place the breadsticks in the air fryer basket.
5. Air fry for 5-7 minutes or until the breadsticks are golden and crispy.
6. Optionally, sprinkle with grated Parmesan cheese before serving.

6. CAPRESE SALAD SKEWERS

 Prep time: 10 minutes   **Servings:** 2

INGREDIENTS:

- 12 cherry tomatoes
- 12 fresh mozzarella balls
- 12 fresh basil leaves
- 2 tablespoons balsamic glaze
- Salt and pepper to taste

NUTRITIONAL INFO (PER SERVING):

Cal: 160 | Carbs: 9g | Pro: 12g
Fat: 9g | Sugars: 7g | Fiber: 2g

INSTRUCTIONS:

1. Thread a cherry tomato, a mozzarella ball, and a basil leaf onto a skewer, and repeat for the remaining skewers.
2. Drizzle balsamic glaze over the skewers.
3. Season with salt and pepper to taste.
4. Serve immediately.

7. STUFFED MUSHROOMS

 Prep time: 15 minutes   **Servings:** 2

INGREDIENTS:

- 8 large white mushrooms
- 1/2 cup cream cheese
- 2 tablespoons grated Parmesan cheese
- 2 cloves garlic, minced
- Salt and pepper to taste

NUTRITIONAL INFO (PER SERVING):

Cal: 190 | Carbs: 5g | Pro: 7g
Fat: 16g | Sugars: 2g | Fiber: 1g

INSTRUCTIONS:

1. Remove the stems from the mushrooms and set them aside.
2. In a bowl, mix the cream cheese, grated Parmesan cheese, minced garlic, salt, and pepper.
3. Stuff each mushroom cap with the cream cheese mixture.
4. Preheat your air fryer to 350°F (175°C).
5. Place the stuffed mushrooms in the air fryer basket.
6. Air fry for 10-12 minutes or until the mushrooms are tender and the filling is golden.

8. AIR FRYER CALAMARI

 Prep time: 15 minutes   **Servings:** 2

INGREDIENTS:

- 1/2 lb (250g) cleaned squid rings
- 1/2 cup breadcrumbs
- 1/4 cup grated Parmesan cheese
- Cooking spray
- Marinara sauce for dipping

NUTRITIONAL INFO (PER SERVING):

Cal: 220 | Carbs: 19g | Pro: 16g
Fat: 9g | Sugars: 1g | Fiber: 1g

INSTRUCTIONS:

1. Preheat your air fryer to 375°F (190°C).
2. In a bowl, mix breadcrumbs and grated Parmesan cheese.
3. Dip each squid ring into the breadcrumb mixture, ensuring they are well-coated.
4. Place the coated calamari in a single layer in the air fryer basket.
5. Lightly spray the calamari with cooking spray.
6. Air fry for 5-7 minutes, or until they are golden and crispy.
7. Serve hot with marinara sauce for dipping.

9. BUFFALO CAULIFLOWER BITES

 Prep time: 10 minutes   **Servings:** 2

INGREDIENTS:

- 1/2 head cauliflower, cut into florets
- 1/2 cup buffalo sauce
- 2 tablespoons melted butter
- Salt and pepper to taste
- Ranch dressing for dipping

NUTRITIONAL INFO (PER SERVING):

Cal: 170 | Carbs: 4g | Pro: 3g
Fat: 16g | Sugars: 1g | Fiber: 2g

INSTRUCTIONS:

1. Preheat your air fryer to 375°F (190°C).
2. In a bowl, mix the buffalo sauce, melted butter, salt, and pepper.
3. Toss the cauliflower florets in the buffalo sauce mixture until they are coated.
4. Place the coated cauliflower in the air fryer basket.
5. Air fry for 12-15 minutes or until the cauliflower is crispy and cooked through.
6. Serve with ranch dressing for dipping.

10. POTATO SKINS WITH BACON AND CHEESE

 Prep time: 15 minutes   **Servings:** 2

INGREDIENTS:

- 2 large russet potatoes
- 4 slices of cooked bacon, crumbled
- 1/2 cup shredded cheddar cheese
- Cooking spray
- Sour cream for dipping

NUTRITIONAL INFO (PER SERVING):

Cal: 320 | Carbs: 28g | Pro: 16g
Fat: 18g | Sugars: 1g | Fiber: 3g

INSTRUCTIONS:

1. Preheat your air fryer to 375°F (190°C).
2. Scrub and dry the potatoes, then rub them with a bit of cooking spray.
3. Place the potatoes in the air fryer and air fry for 35-40 minutes or until they are tender.
4. Remove the potatoes and let them cool slightly.
5. Cut the potatoes in half lengthwise and scoop out the flesh, leaving a thin layer of potato on the skins.
6. Sprinkle crumbled bacon and shredded cheddar cheese on top of the potato skins.
7. Return the potato skins to the air fryer and air fry for an additional 5-7 minutes or until the cheese is melted and bubbly.
8. Serve with sour cream for dipping.

11. SPINACH AND ARTICHOKE DIP

 Prep time: 10 minutes   **Servings:** 2

INGREDIENTS:

- 1 cup frozen chopped spinach, thawed and drained
- 1 cup canned artichoke hearts, drained and chopped
- 1/2 cup mayonnaise
- 1/2 cup grated Parmesan
- Salt and pepper to taste

NUTRITIONAL INFO (PER SERVING):

Cal: 340 | Carbs: 7g | Pro: 9g
Fat: 31g | Sugars: 2g | Fiber: 2g

INSTRUCTIONS:

1. In a bowl, combine the chopped spinach, chopped artichoke hearts, mayonnaise, grated Parmesan cheese, salt, and pepper.
2. Preheat your air fryer to 350°F (175°C).
3. Transfer the mixture into an oven-safe dish that fits in your air fryer.
4. Place the dish in the air fryer basket.
5. Air fry for 12-15 minutes or until the dip is bubbly and lightly browned on top.
6. Serve with tortilla chips or bread slices.

12. LOADED SWEET POTATO NACHOS

 Prep time: 15 minutes   **Servings:** 2

INGREDIENTS:

- 2 medium sweet potatoes, thinly sliced
- 1 cup shredded cheddar cheese
- 1/2 cup black beans, drained and rinsed
- 1/2 cup diced tomatoes
- 1/4 cup sliced green onions

NUTRITIONAL INFO (PER SERVING):

Cal: 400 | Carbs: 45g | Pro: 15g
Fat: 18g | Sugars: 7g | Fiber: 10g

INSTRUCTIONS:

1. Preheat your air fryer to 375°F (190°C).
2. Place the sweet potato slices in a single layer in the air fryer basket.
3. Air fry for 10-12 minutes or until they are crispy.
4. Remove the sweet potato slices from the air fryer and arrange them on a plate.
5. Sprinkle shredded cheddar cheese over the sweet potatoes, and then add black beans and diced tomatoes.
6. Return the plate to the air fryer and air fry for an additional 2-3 minutes, or until the cheese is melted.
7. Garnish with sliced green onions.
8. Serve immediately.

13. ASIAN SPRING ROLLS

 Prep time: 15 minutes   **Servings:** 2

INGREDIENTS:

- 4 spring roll wrappers
- 1 cup shredded lettuce
- 1/2 cup cooked and shredded chicken
- 1/2 cup sliced cucumber
- Hoisin sauce for dipping

NUTRITIONAL INFO (PER SERVING):

Cal: 220 | Carbs: 20g | Pro: 18g
Fat: 7g | Sugars: 5g | Fiber: 3g

INSTRUCTIONS:

1. Lay a damp kitchen towel on your work surface and fill a shallow dish with warm water.
2. Dip a spring roll wrapper into the warm water for about 10 seconds until it becomes soft and pliable.
3. Place the wrapper on the damp towel.
4. Add a handful of shredded lettuce, a portion of shredded chicken, and sliced cucumber in the center of the wrapper.
5. Fold the sides of the wrapper over the filling, then roll up from the bottom to enclose the filling.
6. Repeat for the remaining wrappers.
7. Serve the spring rolls with hoisin sauce for dipping.

14. GARLIC SHRIMP SKEWERS

 Prep time: 10 minutes   **Servings:** 2

INGREDIENTS:

- 12 large shrimp, peeled and deveined
- 2 cloves garlic, minced
- 2 tablespoons olive oil
- Salt and pepper to taste
- Lemon wedges for serving

NUTRITIONAL INFO (PER SERVING):

Cal: 160 | Carbs: 2g | Pro: 18g
Fat: 10g | Sugars: 0g | Fiber: 0g

INSTRUCTIONS:

1. In a bowl, mix the minced garlic, olive oil, salt, and pepper.
2. Thread 6 shrimp onto each skewer.
3. Brush the garlic and oil mixture over the shrimp.
4. Preheat your air fryer to 375°F (190°C).
5. Place the shrimp skewers in the air fryer basket.
6. Air fry for 4-5 minutes per side, or until the shrimp are pink and cooked through.
7. Serve with lemon wedges for squeezing over the shrimp.

15. FRIED PICKLES

 Prep time: 10 minutes   **Servings:** 2

INGREDIENTS:

- 1/2 cup dill pickle slices
- 1/2 cup buttermilk
- 1/2 cup cornmeal
- Cooking spray
- Ranch dressing for dipping

NUTRITIONAL INFO (PER SERVING):

Cal: 140 | Carbs: 22g | Pro: 3g
Fat: 5g | Sugars: 2g | Fiber: 2g

INSTRUCTIONS:

1. In a bowl, soak the pickle slices in buttermilk.
2. Preheat your air fryer to 375°F (190°C).
3. In another bowl, coat the pickles in cornmeal.
4. Place the coated pickles in a single layer in the air fryer basket.
5. Lightly spray the pickles with cooking spray.
6. Air fry for 6-8 minutes or until the pickles are golden and crispy.
7. Serve with ranch dressing for dipping.

16. AVOCADO FRIES WITH CHIPOTLE DIPPING SAUCE

 Prep time: 15 minutes   **Servings:** 2

INGREDIENTS:

- 1 large avocado, sliced into fries
- 1/2 cup breadcrumbs
- 1 egg, beaten
- 1/2 teaspoon chipotle powder
- Cooking spray

For Chipotle Dipping Sauce:

- 1/4 cup mayonnaise
- 1/2 teaspoon chipotle powder
- 1 teaspoon lime juice

INSTRUCTIONS:

1. Preheat your air fryer to 375°F (190°C).
2. Dip each avocado fry in beaten egg, then coat with breadcrumbs mixed with chipotle powder.
3. Place the coated avocado fries in a single layer in the air fryer basket.
4. Lightly spray the fries with cooking spray.
5. Air fry for 7-10 minutes or until they are golden and crispy.
6. In the meantime, mix the mayonnaise, chipotle powder, and lime juice to prepare the dipping sauce.
7. Serve the avocado fries with the chipotle dipping sauce.

NUTRITIONAL INFO (PER SERVING):

Cal: 220 | Carbs: 19g | Pro: 16g Fat: 9g | Sugars: 1g | Fiber: 1g

17. STUFFED BELL PEPPERS

 Prep time: 15 minutes   **Servings:** 2

INGREDIENTS:

- 2 large bell peppers
- 1/2 cup cooked ground beef
- 1/2 cup cooked rice
- 1/2 cup tomato sauce
- Salt and pepper to taste

NUTRITIONAL INFO (PER SERVING):

Cal: 260 | Carbs: 32g | Pro: 14g
Fat: 8g | Sugars: 8g | Fiber: 5g

INSTRUCTIONS:

1. Cut the tops off the bell peppers and remove the seeds and membranes.
2. In a bowl, mix the cooked ground beef, cooked rice, tomato sauce, salt, and pepper.
3. Stuff each bell pepper with the mixture.
4. Preheat your air fryer to 375°F (190°C).
5. Place the stuffed bell peppers in the air fryer basket.
6. Air fry for 25-30 minutes or until the peppers are tender and the filling is heated through.

18. BAKED BRIE WITH CRANBERRY SAUCE

 Prep time: 10 minutes   **Servings:** 2

INGREDIENTS:

- 1 small wheel of Brie cheese
- 1/4 cup cranberry sauce
- 2 tablespoons chopped pecans
- 2 sprigs of fresh rosemary
- Sliced baguette for serving

NUTRITIONAL INFO (PER SERVING):

Cal: 320 | Carbs: 16g | Pro: 16g
Fat: 20g | Sugars: 8g | Fiber: 1g

INSTRUCTIONS:

1. Preheat your air fryer to 350°F (175°C).
2. Place the Brie cheese in an oven-safe dish that fits in your air fryer.
3. Top the Brie with cranberry sauce and chopped pecans.
4. Add fresh rosemary sprigs for flavor.
5. Place the dish in the air fryer basket.
6. Air fry for 8-10 minutes or until the Brie is soft and gooey.
7. Serve with sliced baguette.

19. AIR FRIED MAC AND CHEESE BITES

 Prep time: 15 minutes   **Servings:** 2

INGREDIENTS:

- 1 cup cooked macaroni and cheese, cooled
- 1/2 cup breadcrumbs
- 1 egg, beaten
- Cooking spray
- Marinara sauce for dipping

NUTRITIONAL INFO (PER SERVING):

Cal: 260 | Carbs: 30g | Pro: 8g
Fat: 11g | Sugars: 3g | Fiber: 2g

INSTRUCTIONS:

1. Preheat your air fryer to 375°F (190°C).
2. Take small portions of cooled macaroni and cheese and shape them into bite-sized balls.
3. Dip each mac and cheese bite in beaten egg, then coat with breadcrumbs.
4. Place the coated bites in a single layer in the air fryer basket.
5. Lightly spray the bites with cooking spray.
6. Air fry for 5-7 minutes or until they are golden and crispy.
7. Serve with marinara sauce for dipping.

20. TATER TOT NACHOS

 Prep time: 15 minutes   **Servings:** 2

INGREDIENTS:

- 2 cups frozen tater tots
- 1 cup shredded cheddar cheese
- 1/4 cup diced green onions
- 1/4 cup sour cream
- Salsa for dipping

NUTRITIONAL INFO (PER SERVING):

Cal: 400 | Carbs: 30g | Pro: 10g
Fat: 26g | Sugars: 2g | Fiber: 3g

INSTRUCTIONS:

1. Preheat your air fryer to 375°F (190°C).
2. Place the frozen tater tots in a single layer in the air fryer basket.
3. Air fry for 12-15 minutes or until the tots are crispy.
4. Remove the tots from the air fryer and place them on a plate.
5. Sprinkle shredded cheddar cheese over the tots and return the plate to the air fryer.
6. Air fry for an additional 2-3 minutes or until the cheese is melted.
7. Top with diced green onions.
8. Serve with sour cream and salsa for dipping.

MAIN COURSES

1. CRISPY CHICKEN TENDERS

 Prep time: 15 minutes   **Servings:** 2

INGREDIENTS:

- 2 boneless, skinless chicken breasts, cut into strips
- 1 cup breadcrumbs
- 1 teaspoon paprika
- Salt and pepper to taste
- Cooking spray

NUTRITIONAL INFO (PER SERVING):

Cal: 320 | Carbs: 24g | Pro: 35g
Fat: 7g | Sugars: 2g | Fiber: 2g

INSTRUCTIONS:

1. Preheat your air fryer to 375°F (190°C).
2. In a shallow bowl, combine breadcrumbs, paprika, salt, and pepper.
3. Dip each chicken strip into the breadcrumb mixture, pressing to adhere the crumbs to the chicken.
4. Place the breaded chicken strips in the air fryer basket in a single layer. Do not overcrowd.
5. Lightly spray the chicken strips with cooking spray.
6. Air fry for 12-15 minutes, flipping the tenders halfway through, until they are golden brown and cooked through.

2. AIR FRIED SALMON WITH LEMON BUTTER

 Prep time: 10 minutes   **Servings:** 2

INGREDIENTS:

- 2 salmon fillets
- 2 tablespoons melted butter
- 1 lemon, juiced
- Salt and pepper to taste

NUTRITIONAL INFO (PER SERVING):

Cal: 310 | Carbs: 2g | Pro: 36g
Fat: 18g | Sugars: 1g | Fiber: 0g

INSTRUCTIONS:

1. Preheat your air fryer to 375°F (190°C).
2. Place salmon fillets in the air fryer basket.
3. Drizzle melted butter and lemon juice over the salmon.
4. Season with salt and pepper.
5. Air fry for 10-12 minutes or until the salmon flakes easily with a fork.

3. BBQ PORK CHOPS

 Prep time: 10 minutes   **Servings:** 2

INGREDIENTS:

- 2 pork chops
- 2 tablespoons BBQ sauce
- Salt and pepper to taste

NUTRITIONAL INFO (PER SERVING):

Cal: 260 | Carbs: 5g | Pro: 25g
Fat: 14g | Sugars: 4g | Fiber: 0g

INSTRUCTIONS:

1. Preheat your air fryer to 375°F (190°C).
2. Season the pork chops with salt and pepper.
3. Brush both sides of the pork chops with BBQ sauce.
4. Place the pork chops in the air fryer basket.
5. Air fry for 12-15 minutes, flipping halfway through, until the pork chops are cooked through.

4. COCONUT SHRIMP

 Prep time: 15 minutes   **Servings:** 2

INGREDIENTS:

- 12 large shrimp, peeled and deveined
- 1/2 cup shredded coconut
- 1/4 cup panko breadcrumbs
- Salt and pepper to taste

NUTRITIONAL INFO (PER SERVING):

Cal: 240 | Carbs: 12g | Pro: 12g
Fat: 15g | Sugars: 1g | Fiber: 3g

INSTRUCTIONS:

1. Preheat your air fryer to 375°F (190°C).
2. In a bowl, combine shredded coconut, panko breadcrumbs, salt, and pepper.
3. Dip each shrimp into the mixture, pressing the coating onto the shrimp.
4. Place the coated shrimp in the air fryer basket.
5. Air fry for 6-8 minutes, or until the shrimp are golden and crispy.

5. TERIYAKI CHICKEN SKEWERS

 Prep time: 15 minutes

 Servings: 2

INGREDIENTS:

- 2 boneless, skinless chicken breasts, cut into cubes
- 1/4 cup teriyaki sauce
- 1 tablespoon sesame seeds
- Salt and pepper to taste

NUTRITIONAL INFO (PER SERVING):

Cal: 270 | Carbs: 7g | Pro: 32g
Fat: 10g | Sugars: 6g | Fiber: 1g

INSTRUCTIONS:

1. Preheat your air fryer to 375°F (190°C).
2. Thread the chicken cubes onto skewers.
3. Brush the chicken skewers with teriyaki sauce.
4. Season with salt, pepper, and sesame seeds.
5. Place the skewers in the air fryer basket.
6. Air fry for 10-12 minutes, turning halfway through, until the chicken is cooked through and slightly caramelized.

6. LEMON HERB TILAPIA

 Prep time: 10 minutes

 Servings: 2

INGREDIENTS:

- 2 tilapia fillets
- 2 tablespoons melted butter
- 1 lemon, juiced
- Fresh herbs (such as thyme or rosemary)
- Salt and pepper to taste

NUTRITIONAL INFO (PER SERVING):

Cal: 220 | Carbs: 2g | Pro: 25g
Fat: 12g | Sugars: 1g | Fiber: 0g

INSTRUCTIONS:

1. Preheat your air fryer to 375°F (190°C).
2. Place tilapia fillets in the air fryer basket.
3. Drizzle melted butter and lemon juice over the fillets.
4. Season with salt, pepper, and fresh herbs.
5. Air fry for 8-10 minutes, or until the tilapia is flaky and opaque.

7. AIR FRYER MEATLOAF

 Prep time: 15 minutes   **Servings:** 2

INGREDIENTS:

- 1/2 pound ground beef
- 1/2 cup breadcrumbs
- 1/4 cup ketchup
- Salt and pepper to taste

NUTRITIONAL INFO (PER SERVING):

Cal: 370 | Carbs: 17g | Pro: 20g
Fat: 24g | Sugars: 5g | Fiber: 1g

INSTRUCTIONS:

1. Preheat your air fryer to 375°F (190°C).
2. In a mixing bowl, combine ground beef, breadcrumbs, ketchup, salt, and pepper.
3. Shape the mixture into a mini meatloaf.
4. Place the meatloaf in the air fryer basket.
5. Air fry for 20-25 minutes, or until the meatloaf is cooked through.

8. PANKO-CRUSTED COD

 Prep time: 15 minutes   **Servings:** 2

INGREDIENTS:

- 2 cod fillets
- 1/2 cup panko breadcrumbs
- 1/4 cup grated Parmesan cheese
- Salt and pepper to taste

NUTRITIONAL INFO (PER SERVING):

Cal: 290 | Carbs: 9g | Pro: 30g
Fat: 12g | Sugars: 1g | Fiber: 1g

INSTRUCTIONS:

1. Preheat your air fryer to 375°F (190°C).
2. In a bowl, mix panko breadcrumbs, Parmesan cheese, salt, and pepper.
3. Dip the cod fillets into the breadcrumb mixture, pressing the coating onto the fish.
4. Place the coated cod fillets in the air fryer basket.
5. Air fry for 10-12 minutes or until the cod is crispy and flakes easily.

9. GREEK CHICKEN SOUVLAKI

 Prep time: 15 minutes   **Servings:** 2

INGREDIENTS:

- 2 boneless, skinless chicken breasts, cut into cubes
- 1/4 cup Greek dressing
- 1 teaspoon dried oregano
- Salt and pepper to taste

NUTRITIONAL INFO (PER SERVING):

Cal: 260 | Carbs: 4g | Pro: 30g
Fat: 13g | Sugars: 2g | Fiber: 1g

INSTRUCTIONS:

1. Preheat your air fryer to 375°F (190°C).
2. Thread the chicken cubes onto skewers.
3. Brush the chicken skewers with Greek dressing.
4. Season with dried oregano, salt, and pepper.
5. Place the skewers in the air fryer basket.
6. Air fry for 12-15 minutes, turning halfway through, until the chicken is cooked through and slightly charred.

10. BUFFALO CHICKEN WINGS

 Prep time: 10 minutes   **Servings:** 2

INGREDIENTS:

- 12 chicken wing pieces
- 1/4 cup buffalo wing sauce
- 1 tablespoon melted butter
- Salt and pepper to taste

NUTRITIONAL INFO (PER SERVING):

Cal: 320 | Carbs: 1g | Pro: 22g
Fat: 26g | Sugars: 0g | Fiber: 0g

INSTRUCTIONS:

1. Preheat your air fryer to 375°F (190°C).
2. In a bowl, mix buffalo wing sauce and melted butter.
3. Season the chicken wings with salt and pepper.
4. Toss the wings in the buffalo sauce mixture to coat evenly.
5. Place the coated wings in the air fryer basket.
6. Air fry for 20-25 minutes, turning halfway through, until the wings are crispy and cooked through.

11. BREADED PORK CUTLETS

 Prep time: 15 minutes   **Servings:** 2

INGREDIENTS:

- 2 pork cutlets
- 1/2 cup breadcrumbs
- 1/4 cup grated Parmesan cheese
- Salt and pepper to taste

NUTRITIONAL INFO (PER SERVING):

Cal: 340 | Carbs: 11g | Pro: 37g
Fat: 15g | Sugars: 1g | Fiber: 1g

INSTRUCTIONS:

1. Preheat your air fryer to 375°F (190°C).
2. In a shallow bowl, combine breadcrumbs, Parmesan cheese, salt, and pepper.
3. Dip each pork cutlet into the breadcrumb mixture, pressing the coating onto the cutlets.
4. Place the breaded pork cutlets in the air fryer basket.
5. Air fry for 10-12 minutes, flipping halfway through, until the cutlets are golden and cooked through.

12. AIR FRIED CHICKEN DRUMSTICKS

 Prep time: 15 minutes   **Servings:** 2

INGREDIENTS:

- 4 chicken drumsticks
- 2 tablespoons olive oil
- 1 teaspoon smoked paprika
- Salt and pepper to taste

NUTRITIONAL INFO (PER SERVING):

Cal: 330 | Carbs: 1g | Pro: 22g
Fat: 26g | Sugars: 0g | Fiber: 0g

INSTRUCTIONS:

1. Preheat your air fryer to 375°F (190°C).
2. In a bowl, toss the chicken drumsticks with olive oil, smoked paprika, salt, and pepper.
3. Place the drumsticks in the air fryer basket.
4. Air fry for 20-25 minutes, turning halfway through, until the drumsticks are crispy and cooked through.

13. BEEF AND BROCCOLI

 Prep time: 15 minutes

 Servings: 2

INGREDIENTS:

- 8 oz flank steak, sliced
- 1 cup broccoli florets
- 2 tablespoons soy sauce
- 1 tablespoon honey

NUTRITIONAL INFO (PER SERVING):

Cal: 320 | Carbs: 15g | Pro: 24g
Fat: 16g | Sugars: 10g | Fiber: 2g

INSTRUCTIONS:

1. Preheat your air fryer to 375°F (190°C).
2. In a bowl, mix the sliced steak with soy sauce and honey.
3. Place the marinated steak and broccoli in the air fryer basket.
4. Air fry for 10-12 minutes, tossing halfway through, until the steak is cooked and the broccoli is tender.

14. LEMON GARLIC SHRIMP SCAMPI

 Prep time: 15 minutes

 Servings: 2

INGREDIENTS:

- 12 large shrimp, peeled and deveined
- 2 tablespoons melted butter
- 2 cloves garlic, minced
- Juice of 1 lemon

NUTRITIONAL INFO (PER SERVING):

Cal: 180 | Carbs: 1g | Pro: 12g
Fat: 15g | Sugars: 0g | Fiber: 0g

INSTRUCTIONS:

1. Preheat your air fryer to 375°F (190°C).
2. In a bowl, combine melted butter, minced garlic, and lemon juice.
3. Toss the shrimp in the garlic butter mixture.
4. Place the shrimp in the air fryer basket.
5. Air fry for 6-8 minutes or until the shrimp are pink and opaque.

15. CHICKEN FAJITAS

 Prep time: 15 minutes   **Servings:** 2

INGREDIENTS:

- 2 boneless, skinless chicken breasts, sliced
- 1 red bell pepper, sliced
- 1 onion, sliced
- 2 tablespoons fajita seasoning
- 2 tablespoons olive oil

NUTRITIONAL INFO (PER SERVING):

Cal: 290 | Carbs: 10g | Pro: 28g
Fat: 15g | Sugars: 5g | Fiber: 3g

INSTRUCTIONS:

1. Preheat your air fryer to 375°F (190°C).
2. In a bowl, mix the chicken, bell pepper, onion, fajita seasoning, and olive oil.
3. Place the chicken and vegetable mixture in the air fryer basket.
4. Air fry for 15-18 minutes, tossing halfway through, until the chicken is cooked and the vegetables are tender.

16. PANKO-CRUSTED PORK CHOPS

 Prep time: 15 minutes   **Servings:** 2

INGREDIENTS:

- 2 pork chops
- 1/2 cup panko breadcrumbs
- 1/4 cup grated Parmesan cheese
- Salt and pepper to taste

NUTRITIONAL INFO (PER SERVING):

Cal: 320 | Carbs: 10g | Pro: 31g
Fat: 16g | Sugars: 1g | Fiber: 1g

INSTRUCTIONS:

1. Preheat your air fryer to 375°F (190°C).
2. In a shallow bowl, combine panko breadcrumbs, Parmesan cheese, salt, and pepper.
3. Dip each pork chop into the breadcrumb mixture, pressing the coating onto the chops.
4. Place the breaded pork chops in the air fryer basket.
5. Air fry for 12-15 minutes, flipping halfway through, until the chops are golden and cooked through.

17. CAJUN CATFISH

 Prep time: 15 minutes   **Servings:** 2

INGREDIENTS:

- 2 catfish fillets
- 1 tablespoon Cajun seasoning
- 2 tablespoons olive oil
- Salt and pepper to taste

NUTRITIONAL INFO (PER SERVING):

Cal: 270 | Carbs: 1g | Pro: 21g
Fat: 20g | Sugars: 0g | Fiber: 0g

INSTRUCTIONS:

1. Preheat your air fryer to 375°F (190°C).
2. Season the catfish fillets with Cajun seasoning, salt, and pepper.
3. Drizzle the fillets with olive oil.
4. Place the catfish in the air fryer basket.
5. Air fry for 10-12 minutes, or until the catfish is flaky and well-seasoned.

18. CRISPY TOFU STIR-FRY

 Prep time: 15 minutes   **Servings:** 2

INGREDIENTS:

- 8 oz firm tofu, cubed
- 1 cup mixed stir-fry vegetables
- 2 tablespoons soy sauce
- 1 tablespoon sesame oil

NUTRITIONAL INFO (PER SERVING):

Cal: 250 | Carbs: 10g | Pro: 14g
Fat: 16g | Sugars: 3g | Fiber: 3g

INSTRUCTIONS:

1. Preheat your air fryer to 375°F (190°C).
2. Toss the tofu and mixed vegetables with soy sauce and sesame oil.
3. Place the tofu and vegetables in the air fryer basket.
4. Air fry for 15-18 minutes, shaking the basket occasionally, until the tofu is crispy and the vegetables are tender.

19. LEMON PEPPER CHICKEN

 Prep time: 15 minutes   **Servings:** 2

INGREDIENTS:

- 2 boneless, skinless chicken breasts
- 2 tablespoons olive oil
- Zest of 1 lemon
- Salt and pepper to taste

NUTRITIONAL INFO (PER SERVING):

Cal: 270 | Carbs: 0g | Pro: 26g
Fat: 18g | Sugars: 0g | Fiber: 0g

INSTRUCTIONS:

1. Preheat your air fryer to 375°F (190°C).
2. Rub the chicken breasts with olive oil, lemon zest, salt, and pepper.
3. Place the chicken breasts in the air fryer basket.
4. Air fry for 12-15 minutes, turning halfway through, until the chicken is cooked through and lightly browned.

20. AIR FRYER VEGGIE BURGERS

 Prep time: 15 minutes   **Servings:** 2

INGREDIENTS:

- 2 veggie burger patties
- 2 whole wheat burger buns
- 2 slices of cheese (optional)
- Lettuce and tomato for garnish
- Ketchup and mustard for serving

NUTRITIONAL INFO (PER SERVING):

Cal: 320 | Carbs: 50g | Pro: 15g
Fat: 8g | Sugars: 7g | Fiber: 10g

INSTRUCTIONS:

1. Preheat your air fryer to 375°F (190°C).
2. Place the veggie burger patties in the air fryer basket.
3. Air fry for 8-10 minutes, or until heated through and slightly crispy.
4. If desired, place a slice of cheese on each patty and air fry for an additional minute to melt.
5. Toast the burger buns in the air fryer for 1-2 minutes.
6. Assemble the burgers with lettuce, tomato, and condiments as desired.

POULTRY

1. CHICKEN PARMESAN

 Prep time: 10 minutes   **Servings:** 2

INGREDIENTS:

- 2 boneless, skinless chicken breasts
- 1 cup marinara sauce
- 1 cup shredded mozzarella cheese
- 1/2 cup bread crumbs
- Olive oil cooking spray

NUTRITIONAL INFO (PER SERVING):

Cal: 520 | Carbs: 21g | Pro: 54g
Fat: 24g | Sugars: 6g | Fiber: 2g

INSTRUCTIONS:

1. Preheat the air fryer to 375°F (190°C).
2. Dredge each chicken breast in bread crumbs, ensuring they are evenly coated.
3. Place the breaded chicken breasts in the air fryer basket, ensuring they're not touching.
4. Cook for 10 minutes, flipping halfway through, or until the chicken reaches an internal temperature of 165°F (74°C).
5. Spoon marinara sauce over each chicken breast and sprinkle with mozzarella cheese.
6. Return to the air fryer for an additional 2-3 minutes until the cheese is bubbly and golden brown.
7. Serve hot, over pasta or with a side salad.

2. HONEY MUSTARD CHICKEN TENDERS

 Prep time: 10 minutes   **Servings:** 2

INGREDIENTS:

- 1/4 cup honey mustard sauce
- 1/2 cup bread crumbs
- Olive oil cooking spray

NUTRITIONAL INFO (PER SERVING):

Cal: 375 | Carbs: 17g | Pro: 30g
Fat: 20g | Sugars: 6g | Fiber: 1g

INSTRUCTIONS:

1. Preheat the air fryer to 375°F (190°C).
2. Coat chicken tenders with honey mustard sauce.
3. Dredge each tender in bread crumbs to coat evenly.
4. Place the tenders in the air fryer basket, ensuring they're not touching.
5. Cook for 8-10 minutes, flipping halfway through, until golden and crispy.
6. Serve with extra honey mustard for dipping.

3. CRISPY BUFFALO CHICKEN SANDWICH

 Prep time: 15 minutes

 Servings: 2

INGREDIENTS:

- 2 boneless chicken breasts
- 1/2 cup buffalo sauce
- 1/2 cup bread crumbs
- 2 hamburger buns
- Olive oil cooking spray

NUTRITIONAL INFO (PER SERVING):

Cal: 470 | Carbs: 39g | Pro: 31g
Fat: 18g | Sugars: 3g | Fiber: 2g

INSTRUCTIONS:

1. Preheat the air fryer to 375°F (190°C).
2. Coat chicken breasts with buffalo sauce.
3. Dredge each breast in bread crumbs to coat evenly.
4. Place the chicken in the air fryer basket and cook for 12-15 minutes, flipping halfway through, until chicken is cooked through and crispy.
5. Serve on hamburger buns with your favorite toppings.

4. COCONUT CURRY CHICKEN

 Prep time: 10 minutes

 Servings: 2

INGREDIENTS:

- 2 boneless chicken breasts
- 1/2 cup coconut milk
- 2 tbsp red curry paste
- 1 tbsp oil
- Salt and pepper to taste

NUTRITIONAL INFO (PER SERVING):

Cal: 385 | Carbs: 8g | Pro: 28g
Fat: 27g | Sugars: 2g | Fiber: 1g

INSTRUCTIONS:

1. Preheat the air fryer to 375°F (190°C).
2. Season chicken breasts with salt and pepper.
3. In a bowl, mix coconut milk and red curry paste.
4. Coat chicken with the curry mixture.
5. Place the chicken in the air fryer basket and cook for 12-15 minutes, or until the chicken reaches an internal temperature of 165°F (74°C).
6. Serve with rice and extra sauce.

5. LEMON HERB CHICKEN THIGHS

 Prep time: 10 minutes   **Servings:** 2

INGREDIENTS:

- 4 chicken thighs
- 2 tbsp lemon juice
- 2 tsp dried herbs (thyme, rosemary, oregano)
- Salt and pepper to taste

NUTRITIONAL INFO (PER SERVING):

Cal: 290 | Carbs: 2g | Pro: 28g
Fat: 19g | Sugars: 0g | Fiber: 1g

INSTRUCTIONS:

1. Preheat the air fryer to 375°F (190°C).
2. Season chicken thighs with salt, pepper, and dried herbs.
3. Drizzle lemon juice over the chicken.
4. Place the chicken in the air fryer basket and cook for 20-25 minutes or until chicken is cooked through and skin is crispy.
5. Serve with your favorite side dishes.

6. BACON-WRAPPED CHICKEN BITES

 Prep time: 10 minutes   **Servings:** 2

INGREDIENTS:

- 4 boneless chicken tenders
- 4 slices of bacon
- Salt and pepper to taste
- Toothpicks

NUTRITIONAL INFO (PER SERVING):

Cal: 340 | Carbs: 0g | Pro: 34g
Fat: 23g | Sugars: 0g | Fiber: 0g

INSTRUCTIONS:

1. Preheat the air fryer to 375°F (190°C).
2. Season chicken tenders with salt and pepper.
3. Wrap each tender with a slice of bacon and secure with toothpicks.
4. Place the bacon-wrapped chicken in the air fryer basket and cook for 12-15 minutes, turning halfway, until bacon is crispy and chicken is cooked through.
5. Serve as an appetizer or with a side salad.

7. GARLIC PARMESAN CHICKEN WINGS

 Prep time: 10 minutes

 Servings: 2

INGREDIENTS:

- 8 chicken wings
- 1/4 cup grated Parmesan cheese
- 2 tsp minced garlic
- Salt and pepper to taste

NUTRITIONAL INFO (PER SERVING):

Cal: 350 | Carbs: 2g | Pro: 30g
Fat: 24g | Sugars: 0g | Fiber: 0g

INSTRUCTIONS:

1. Preheat the air fryer to 375°F (190°C).
2. Season chicken wings with salt, pepper, and minced garlic.
3. Coat the wings with grated Parmesan cheese.
4. Place the wings in the air fryer basket and cook for 18-20 minutes, turning once, until wings are crispy and fully cooked.
5. Serve with your favorite dipping sauce.

8. TERIYAKI TURKEY MEATBALLS

 Prep time: 15 minutes

 Servings: 2

INGREDIENTS:

- 8 turkey meatballs
- 1/4 cup teriyaki sauce
- 1/4 cup pineapple chunks
- 1/4 cup red bell pepper chunks

NUTRITIONAL INFO (PER SERVING):

Cal: 340 | Carbs: 20g | Pro: 20g
Fat: 19g | Sugars: 15g | Fiber: 2g

INSTRUCTIONS:

1. Preheat the air fryer to 375°F (190°C).
2. In a bowl, mix teriyaki sauce, pineapple, and red bell pepper.
3. Coat turkey meatballs with the teriyaki mixture.
4. Place the meatballs in the air fryer basket and cook for 12-15 minutes, shaking the basket occasionally, until meatballs are heated through and sauce is caramelized.
5. Serve over rice or as an appetizer with toothpicks.

9. MEDITERRANEAN CHICKEN SKEWERS

 Prep time: 15 minutes   **Servings:** 2

INGREDIENTS:

- 8 chicken breast chunks
- 2 tbsp olive oil
- 2 tsp Mediterranean seasoning blend
- 1/4 cup plain Greek yogurt

NUTRITIONAL INFO (PER SERVING):

Cal: 340 | Carbs: 2g | Pro: 30g
Fat: 22g | Sugars: 0g | Fiber: 0g

INSTRUCTIONS:

1. Preheat the air fryer to 375°F (190°C).
2. In a bowl, mix olive oil and Mediterranean seasoning blend.
3. Coat chicken chunks with the seasoning mixture.
4. Thread chicken onto skewers.
5. Place the skewers in the air fryer basket and cook for 12-15 minutes, turning halfway through, until chicken is cooked through.
6. Serve with a side of Greek yogurt.

10. PESTO STUFFED CHICKEN BREASTS

 Prep time: 10 minutes   **Servings:** 2

INGREDIENTS:

- 2 boneless chicken breasts
- 1/4 cup pesto sauce
- Salt and pepper to taste

NUTRITIONAL INFO (PER SERVING):

Cal: 350 | Carbs: 2g | Pro: 30g
Fat: 23g | Sugars: 0g | Fiber: 0g

INSTRUCTIONS:

1. Preheat the air fryer to 375°F (190°C).
2. Make a pocket in each chicken breast by slicing horizontally, being careful not to cut all the way through.
3. Season chicken breasts with salt and pepper.
4. Stuff each breast with pesto sauce.
5. Place the stuffed chicken breasts in the air fryer basket and cook for 20-25 minutes, or until the chicken reaches an internal temperature of 165°F (74°C).
6. Serve with your favorite side dishes.

11. ORANGE GLAZED DUCK BREAST

 Prep time: 10 minutes   **Servings:** 2

INGREDIENTS:

- 2 duck breasts
- 1/4 cup orange marmalade
- 1 tbsp soy sauce
- Salt and pepper to taste

NUTRITIONAL INFO (PER SERVING):

Cal: 350 | Carbs: 18g | Pro: 23g
Fat: 18g | Sugars: 16g | Fiber: 0g

INSTRUCTIONS:

1. Preheat the air fryer to 375°F (190°C).
2. Season duck breasts with salt and pepper.
3. In a small bowl, mix orange marmalade and soy sauce.
4. Coat duck breasts with the glaze.
5. Place the duck breasts in the air fryer basket and cook for 12-15 minutes, turning once, until duck is cooked to your desired level of doneness.
6. Serve with extra glaze as a dipping sauce.

12. RANCH CHICKEN TENDERS

 Prep time: 10 minutes   **Servings:** 2

INGREDIENTS:

- 8 chicken tenders
- 1/4 cup ranch dressing
- 1/2 cup bread crumbs
- Olive oil cooking spray

NUTRITIONAL INFO (PER SERVING):

Cal: 400 | Carbs: 18g | Pro: 30g
Fat: 23g | Sugars: 2g | Fiber: 1g

INSTRUCTIONS:

1. Preheat the air fryer to 375°F (190°C).
2. Coat chicken tenders with ranch dressing.
3. Dredge each tender in bread crumbs to coat evenly.
4. Place the tenders in the air fryer basket and cook for 8-10 minutes, flipping halfway through, until golden and crispy.
5. Serve with extra ranch for dipping.

13. BBQ CHICKEN DRUMETTES

 Prep time: 10 minutes

 Servings: 2

INGREDIENTS:

- 8 chicken drumettes
- 1/4 cup BBQ sauce
- Salt and pepper to taste

NUTRITIONAL INFO (PER SERVING):

Cal: 330 | Carbs: 16g | Pro: 20g
Fat: 21g | Sugars: 12g | Fiber: 0g

INSTRUCTIONS:

1. Preheat the air fryer to 375°F (190°C).
2. Season chicken drumettes with salt and pepper.
3. Coat drumettes with BBQ sauce.
4. Place the drumettes in the air fryer basket and cook for 15-18 minutes, turning occasionally, until the chicken is cooked through and the sauce is caramelized.
5. Serve with extra BBQ sauce for dipping.

14. SESAME GINGER CHICKEN

 Prep time: 10 minutes

 Servings: 2

INGREDIENTS:

- 2 boneless chicken breasts
- 2 tbsp sesame ginger sauce
- 2 tbsp sesame seeds
- Salt and pepper to taste

NUTRITIONAL INFO (PER SERVING):

Cal: 320 | Carbs: 4g | Pro: 28g
Fat: 18g | Sugars: 1g | Fiber: 2g

INSTRUCTIONS:

1. Preheat the air fryer to 375°F (190°C).
2. Season chicken breasts with salt and pepper.
3. Coat chicken with sesame ginger sauce.
4. Sprinkle sesame seeds over the chicken.
5. Place the chicken in the air fryer basket and cook for 15-20 minutes, or until chicken is fully cooked and the sesame seeds are golden and toasted.
6. Serve with your choice of side dishes.

15. CHICKEN AND CHORIZO SKEWERS

 Prep time: 15 minutes   **Servings:** 2

INGREDIENTS:

- 8 chicken breast chunks
- 1/4 cup chorizo sausage, sliced
- 2 tbsp olive oil
- Salt and pepper to taste

NUTRITIONAL INFO (PER SERVING):

Cal: 380 | Carbs: 2g | Pro: 30g
Fat: 28g | Sugars: 1g | Fiber: 0g

INSTRUCTIONS:

1. Preheat the air fryer to 375°F (190°C).
2. Season chicken chunks with salt and pepper.
3. Thread chicken and chorizo onto skewers.
4. Brush skewers with olive oil.
5. Place the skewers in the air fryer basket and cook for 12-15 minutes, turning halfway through, until chicken is cooked through.
6. Serve with your favorite side dishes.

16. MAPLE GLAZED DUCK LEGS

 Prep time: 10 minutes   **Servings:** 2

INGREDIENTS:

- 2 duck legs
- 1/4 cup maple syrup
- 1 tsp Dijon mustard
- Salt and pepper to taste

NUTRITIONAL INFO (PER SERVING):

Cal: 380 | Carbs: 28g | Pro: 19g
Fat: 24g | Sugars: 25g | Fiber: 0g

INSTRUCTIONS:

1. Preheat the air fryer to 375°F (190°C).
2. Season duck legs with salt and pepper.
3. In a bowl, mix maple syrup and Dijon mustard.
4. Coat duck legs with the maple glaze.
5. Place the duck legs in the air fryer basket and cook for 20-25 minutes, turning once, until duck is cooked to your desired level of doneness and the glaze is caramelized.
6. Serve with your favorite side dishes.

17. ROSEMARY ROASTED CORNISH HENS

 Prep time: 10 minutes   **Servings:** 2

INGREDIENTS:

- 2 Cornish hens
- 2 tsp fresh rosemary, chopped
- 2 tbsp olive oil
- Salt and pepper to taste

NUTRITIONAL INFO (PER SERVING):

Cal: 430 | Carbs: 0g | Pro: 38g
Fat: 29g | Sugars: 0g | Fiber: 0g

INSTRUCTIONS:

1. Preheat the air fryer to 375°F (190°C).
2. Season Cornish hens with salt, pepper, and chopped rosemary.
3. Brush hens with olive oil.
4. Place the hens in the air fryer basket and cook for 30-35 minutes, or until they reach an internal temperature of 165°F (74°C) and the skin is crispy.
5. Serve with your favorite side dishes.

18. HONEY SRIRACHA CHICKEN

 Prep time: 10 minutes   **Servings:** 2

INGREDIENTS:

- 2 boneless chicken breasts
- 2 tbsp honey
- 2 tbsp Sriracha sauce
- Salt and pepper to taste

NUTRITIONAL INFO (PER SERVING):

Cal: 340 | Carbs: 18g | Pro: 30g
Fat: 18g | Sugars: 17g | Fiber: 0g

INSTRUCTIONS:

1. Preheat the air fryer to 375°F (190°C).
2. Season chicken breasts with salt and pepper.
3. In a bowl, mix honey and Sriracha sauce.
4. Coat chicken with the honey Sriracha mixture.
5. Place the chicken in the air fryer basket and cook for 12-15 minutes, or until chicken is fully cooked and has a sticky glaze.
6. Serve with your choice of side dishes.

19. CAJUN TURKEY LEGS

 Prep time: 10 minutes   **Servings:** 2

INGREDIENTS:

- 2 turkey legs
- 2 tsp Cajun seasoning
- 1 tbsp oil
- Salt and pepper to taste

NUTRITIONAL INFO (PER SERVING):

Cal: 340 | Carbs: 0g | Pro: 24g
Fat: 27g | Sugars: 0g | Fiber: 0g

INSTRUCTIONS:

1. Preheat the air fryer to 375°F (190°C).
2. Season turkey legs with salt, pepper, and Cajun seasoning.
3. Brush turkey legs with oil.
4. Place the turkey legs in the air fryer basket and cook for 30-35 minutes, turning occasionally, until the turkey legs are cooked through and the skin is crispy.
5. Serve with your favorite side dishes.

20. AIR FRIED QUAIL

 Prep time: 10 minutes   **Servings:** 2

INGREDIENTS:

- 4 quail
- 2 tsp paprika
- 2 tbsp olive oil
- Salt and pepper to taste

NUTRITIONAL INFO (PER SERVING):

Cal: 350 | Carbs: 0g | Pro: 30g
Fat: 23g | Sugars: 0g | Fiber: 0g

INSTRUCTIONS:

1.
2. Preheat the air fryer to 375°F (190°C).
3. Season quail with salt, pepper, and paprika.
4. Brush quail with olive oil.
5. Place the quail in the air fryer basket and cook for 12-15 minutes, turning occasionally, until the quail are cooked through and the skin is crispy.
6. Serve with your choice of side dishes.

BEEF AND PORK

1. BEEF AND BROCCOLI

 Prep time: 10 minutes   **Servings:** 2

INGREDIENTS:

- 8 oz beef sirloin, thinly sliced
- 2 cups broccoli florets
- 2 tablespoons soy sauce
- 2 tablespoons brown sugar
- 1 teaspoon minced garlic

NUTRITIONAL INFO (PER SERVING):

Cal: 250 | Carbs: 16g | Pro: 26g
Fat: 8g | Sugars: 10g | Fiber: 2g

INSTRUCTIONS:

1. In a bowl, combine the soy sauce, brown sugar, and minced garlic.
2. Toss the sliced beef in the sauce and let it marinate for 5 minutes.
3. Place the marinated beef and broccoli in the air fryer basket.
4. Air fry at 375°F (190°C) for 10-12 minutes, or until the beef is cooked and the broccoli is tender.
5. Serve over rice.

2. BACON-WRAPPED FILET MIGNON

 Prep time: 5 minutes   **Servings:** 2

INGREDIENTS:

- 2 filet mignon steaks
- 4 slices of bacon
- 1/2 teaspoon salt
- 1/2 teaspoon black pepper

NUTRITIONAL INFO (PER SERVING):

Cal: 400 | Carbs: 1g | Pro: 30g
Fat: 31g | Sugars: 0g | Fiber: 0g

INSTRUCTIONS:

1. Season the filet mignon steaks with salt and pepper.
2. Wrap 2 slices of bacon around each steak and secure with toothpicks.
3. Place the steaks in the air fryer basket.
4. Air fry at 400°F (200°C) for 12-15 minutes for medium-rare, or longer for desired doneness.
5. Let rest for a few minutes before serving.

3. AIR FRYER PORK CHOPS

 Prep time: 10 minutes   **Servings:** 2

INGREDIENTS:

- 2 pork chops
- 2 tablespoons olive oil
- 1 teaspoon paprika
- 1 teaspoon garlic powder

NUTRITIONAL INFO (PER SERVING):

Cal: 300 | Carbs: 1g | Pro: 32g
Fat: 18g | Sugars: 0g | Fiber: 0g

INSTRUCTIONS:

1. Brush the pork chops with olive oil and sprinkle with paprika and garlic powder.
2. Place the pork chops in the air fryer basket.
3. Air fry at 375°F (190°C) for 12-15 minutes, flipping halfway through, until the pork chops reach an internal temperature of 145°F (63°C).
4. Let them rest for a few minutes before serving.

4. ITALIAN MEATBALLS

 Prep time: 10 minutes   **Servings:** 2

INGREDIENTS:

- 6 Italian meatballs (precooked)
- 1 cup marinara sauce
- 1/2 cup shredded mozzarella cheese
- 1/2 teaspoon dried oregano

INSTRUCTIONS:

1. Place the precooked meatballs in the air fryer basket.
2. Spoon marinara sauce over the meatballs and sprinkle with mozzarella cheese and oregano.
3. Air fry at 375°F (190°C) for 8-10 minutes, or until the meatballs are heated through, and the cheese is melted and bubbly.
4. Serve with your favorite side.

NUTRITIONAL INFO (PER SERVING):

Cal: 450 | Carbs: 8g | Pro: 26g
Fat: 34g | Sugars: 4g | Fiber: 2g

5. CRISPY PORK BELLY BITES

 Prep time: 5 minutes   **Servings:** 2

INGREDIENTS:

- 8 oz pork belly, cubed
- 1 tablespoon soy sauce
- 1 teaspoon Chinese fi-ve-spice powder
- 1/2 teaspoon salt

NUTRITIONAL INFO (PER SERVING):

Cal: 450 | Carbs: 1g | Pro: 11g
Fat: 43g | Sugars: 0g | Fiber: 0g

INSTRUCTIONS:

1. Toss the pork belly cubes in soy sauce, Chinese five-spice pow-der, and salt.
2. Place the pork belly in the air fryer basket.
3. Air fry at 375°F (190°C) for 15-18 minutes, or until the pork belly is crispy and cooked through.
4. Serve as a delicious appetizer or side dish.

6. STUFFED BELL PEPPERS

 Prep time: 10 minutes   **Servings:** 2

INGREDIENTS:

- 2 bell peppers
- 1 cup cooked ground beef (seasoned)
- 1/2 cup cooked rice
- 1/2 cup tomato sauce
- 1/2 cup shredded cheddar cheese

NUTRITIONAL INFO (PER SERVING):

Cal: 400 | Carbs: 23g | Pro: 22g
Fat: 24g | Sugars: 9g | Fiber: 4g

INSTRUCTIONS:

1. Cut the tops off the bell peppers and remove the seeds.
2. Fill the bell peppers with a mixture of cooked ground beef and rice.
3. Top with tomato sauce and shredded cheddar cheese.
4. Place the stuffed bell peppers in the air fryer basket.
5. Air fry at 375°F (190°C) for 15-20 minutes, or until the peppers are tender and the cheese is melted and bubbly.
6. Serve with additional tomato sauce, if desired.

7. BEEF KABOBS

 Prep time: 15 minutes   **Servings:** 2

INGREDIENTS:

- 8 oz beef sirloin, cut into cubes
- 1/2 red bell pepper, cut into chunks
- 1/2 green bell pepper, cut into chunks
- 1/2 red onion, cut into chunks
- 2 tablespoons teriyaki sauce

INSTRUCTIONS:

1. Thread the beef cubes, bell pepper, and onion onto skewers, alternating between them.
2. Brush the kabobs with teriyaki sauce.
3. Place the beef kabobs in the air fryer basket.
4. Air fry at 375°F (190°C) for 12-15 minutes, turning them halfway through, or until the beef is cooked to your desired level of doneness and the vegetables are tender.
5. Serve with rice or a side salad.

NUTRITIONAL INFO (PER SERVING):

Cal: 350 | Carbs: 14g | Pro: 28g | Fat: 18g | Sugars: 10g
Fiber: 3g

8. PORK TENDERLOIN MEDALLIONS

 Prep time: 10 minutes   **Servings:** 2

INGREDIENTS:

- 12 oz pork tenderloin, sliced into medallions
- 1 tablespoon olive oil
- 1 teaspoon garlic powder
- 1/2 teaspoon paprika

NUTRITIONAL INFO (PER SERVING):

Cal: 280 | Carbs: 1g | Pro: 34g
Fat: 14g | Sugars: 0g | Fiber: 0g

INSTRUCTIONS:

1. Brush the pork tenderloin medallions with olive oil and sprinkle with garlic powder and paprika.
2. Place the medallions in the air fryer basket.
3. Air fry at 375°F (190°C) for 10-12 minutes, turning halfway through, until the pork is cooked to an internal temperature of 145°F (63°C).
4. Serve with your choice of sides.

9. TERIYAKI BEEF SKEWERS

 Prep time: 15 minutes   **Servings:** 2

INGREDIENTS:

- 8 oz beef sirloin, cut into cubes
- 1/4 cup teriyaki sauce
- 1/2 red bell pepper, cut into chunks
- 1/2 green bell pepper, cut into chunks

NUTRITIONAL INFO (PER SERVING):

Cal: 280 | Carbs: 8g | Pro: 25g
Fat: 14g | Sugars: 6g | Fiber: 2g

INSTRUCTIONS:

1. In a bowl, marinate the beef cubes in teriyaki sauce for 10 minutes.
2. Thread the marinated beef cubes and bell pepper chunks onto skewers, alternating between them.
3. Place the beef skewers in the air fryer basket.
4. Air fry at 375°F (190°C) for 10-12 minutes, turning them halfway through, or until the beef is cooked to your desired level of doneness and the peppers are tender.
5. Serve with rice or noodles.

10. BBQ PORK RIBS

 Prep time: 10 minutes   **Servings:** 2

INGREDIENTS:

- 1 lb pork ribs
- 1/4 cup barbecue sauce
- 1/2 teaspoon smoked paprika
- 1/2 teaspoon salt

NUTRITIONAL INFO (PER SERVING):

Cal: 450 | Carbs: 10g | Pro: 25g
Fat: 32g | Sugars: 8g | Fiber: 0g

INSTRUCTIONS:

1. Season the pork ribs with smoked paprika and salt.
2. Brush the ribs with barbecue sauce.
3. Place the ribs in the air fryer basket.
4. Air fry at 350°F (175°C) for 25-30 minutes, turning and basting with more sauce halfway through, or until the ribs are cooked and tender.
5. Serve with your favorite sides.

11. CRISPY BEEF TACOS

 Prep time: 15 minutes   **Servings:** 2

INGREDIENTS:

- 8 oz ground beef
- 1/2 cup shredded cheddar cheese
- 4 small flour tortillas
- 1/2 cup salsa

NUTRITIONAL INFO (PER SERVING):

Cal: 450 | Carbs: 23g | Pro: 25g
Fat: 28g | Sugars: 3g | Fiber: 2g

INSTRUCTIONS:

1. Cook the ground beef in a skillet until browned and crumbled.
2. Warm the flour tortillas in the air fryer for 2 minutes at 350°F (175°C).
3. Place the cooked beef, shredded cheddar cheese, and salsa on the tortillas.
4. Fold the tortillas to make tacos.
5. Air fry the tacos at 375°F (190°C) for 5 minutes, or until the cheese is melted, and the tacos are crispy.
6. Serve with your favorite toppings.

12. GARLIC BUTTER STEAK BITES

 Prep time: 10 minutes   **Servings:** 2

INGREDIENTS:

- 8 oz sirloin steak, cut into cubes
- 2 tablespoons melted butter
- 2 cloves garlic, minced
- 1/2 teaspoon chopped fresh parsley

NUTRITIONAL INFO (PER SERVING):

Cal: 320 | Carbs: 1g | Pro: 22g
Fat: 26g | Sugars: 0g | Fiber: 0g

INSTRUCTIONS:

1. In a bowl, combine melted butter, minced garlic, and chopped parsley.
2. Toss the steak cubes in the garlic butter mixture.
3. Place the steak bites in the air fryer basket.
4. Air fry at 400°F (200°C) for 8-10 minutes, or until the steak is cooked to your desired level of doneness.
5. Serve with a side salad or vegetables.

13. PORK AND APPLE SLIDERS

 Prep time: 15 minutes   **Servings:** 2

INGREDIENTS:

- 2 small pork tenderloin medallions
- 2 small dinner rolls
- 1 small apple, thinly sliced
- 2 tablespoons honey

NUTRITIONAL INFO (PER SERVING):

Cal: 350 | Carbs: 39g | Pro: 13g
Fat: 15g | Sugars: 21g | Fiber: 2g

INSTRUCTIONS:

1. Air fry the pork tenderloin medallions at 375°F (190°C) for 10-12 minutes, turning once, until cooked to an internal temperature of 145°F (63°C).
2. Slice the dinner rolls in half and lightly toast them in the air fryer for 2 minutes.
3. Assemble the sliders by placing the cooked pork, apple slices, and drizzle honey on the toasted rolls.
4. Serve with your favorite side.

14. KOREAN BBQ SHORT RIBS

 Prep time: 15 minutes   **Servings:** 2

INGREDIENTS:

- 4 Korean short ribs
- 2 tablespoons soy sauce
- 1 tablespoon brown sugar
- 1 teaspoon minced garlic

NUTRITIONAL INFO (PER SERVING):

Cal: 350 | Carbs: 7g | Pro: 25g
Fat: 24g | Sugars: 6g | Fiber: 0g

INSTRUCTIONS:

1. In a bowl, mix soy sauce, brown sugar, and minced garlic to create a marinade.
2. Coat the short ribs with the marinade and let them marinate for 10 minutes.
3. Place the marinated short ribs in the air fryer basket.
4. Air fry at 375°F (190°C) for 8-10 minutes, turning once, or until the short ribs are cooked and slightly caramelized.
5. Serve with rice and your favorite veggies.

15. SALISBURY STEAK

 Prep time: 10 minutes   **Servings:** 2

INGREDIENTS:

- 8 oz ground beef
- 1/4 cup bread crumbs
- 1/4 cup beef broth
- 1/4 cup diced onions
- 1/4 cup mushroom slices

NUTRITIONAL INFO (PER SERVING):

Cal: 350 | Carbs: 15g | Pro: 25g
Fat: 20g | Sugars: 2g | Fiber: 2g

INSTRUCTIONS:

1. In a bowl, mix ground beef, bread crumbs, diced onions, and beef broth.
2. Shape the mixture into two oval patties.
3. Place the patties in the air fryer basket and top with mushroom slices.
4. Air fry at 375°F (190°C) for 10-12 minutes, or until the patties are cooked through.
5. Serve with mashed potatoes or a side of your choice.

16. PULLED PORK SANDWICHES

 Prep time: 10 minutes   **Servings:** 2

INGREDIENTS:

- 8 oz pulled pork (precooked)
- 2 hamburger buns
- 1/2 cup coleslaw
- 2 tablespoons barbecue sauce

NUTRITIONAL INFO (PER SERVING):

Cal: 450 | Carbs: 35g | Pro: 24g
Fat: 23g | Sugars: 12g | Fiber: 3g

INSTRUCTIONS:

1. Place the precooked pulled pork in the air fryer basket.
2. Air fry at 375°F (190°C) for 8-10 minutes, or until the pork is heated through.
3. Toast the hamburger buns in the air fryer for 2 minutes.
4. Assemble the sandwiches by placing the pulled pork on the buns and topping with coleslaw and barbecue sauce.
5. Serve with a side of chips or fries.

17. SOUTHWEST BEEF BURRITOS

 Prep time: 15 minutes

 Servings: 2

INGREDIENTS:

- 8 oz ground beef, cooked and seasoned
- 2 small flour tortillas
- 1/2 cup black beans
- 1/2 cup shredded cheddar cheese

NUTRITIONAL INFO (PER SERVING):

Cal: 400 | Carbs: 25g | Pro: 23g
Fat: 24g | Sugars: 2g | Fiber: 4g

INSTRUCTIONS:

1. Warm the flour tortillas in the air fryer for 2 minutes at 350°F (175°C).
2. Fill each tortilla with cooked ground beef, black beans, and shredded cheddar cheese.
3. Fold the tortillas to make burritos.
4. Air fry the burritos at 375°F (190°C) for 5 minutes, or until the cheese is melted, and the burritos are heated through.
5. Serve with salsa or sour cream.

18. PORK AND PINEAPPLE SKEWERS

 Prep time: 15 minutes

 Servings: 2

INGREDIENTS:

- 8 oz pork loin, cut into cubes
- 1/2 cup pineapple chunks
- 1/4 cup teriyaki sauce
- 1/4 teaspoon ground ginger

NUTRITIONAL INFO (PER SERVING):

Cal: 350 | Carbs: 20g | Pro: 25g
Fat: 15g | Sugars: 16g | Fiber: 2g

INSTRUCTIONS:

1. In a bowl, mix teriyaki sauce and ground ginger to create a marinade.
2. Thread the pork cubes and pineapple chunks onto skewers.
3. Brush the skewers with the teriyaki marinade.
4. Place the skewers in the air fryer basket.
5. Air fry at 375°F (190°C) for 10-12 minutes, turning them halfway through, until the pork is cooked and the pineapple is caramelized.
6. Serve with rice.

19. PHILLY CHEESESTEAK EGG ROLLS

 Prep time: 15 minutes   **Servings:** 2

INGREDIENTS:

- 4 egg roll wrappers
- 4 oz thinly sliced beef steak
- 1/2 cup sliced bell peppers
- 1/2 cup sliced onions

NUTRITIONAL INFO (PER SERVING):

Cal: 320 | Carbs: 34g | Pro: 18g
Fat: 12g | Sugars: 5g | Fiber: 2g

INSTRUCTIONS:

1. Place the beef steak, bell peppers, and onions in a bowl and toss to combine.
2. Lay out an egg roll wrapper and place a portion of the mixture in the center.
3. Fold in the sides and roll up the wrapper, sealing the edges with a little water.
4. Repeat for the remaining wrappers and filling.
5. Place the egg rolls in the air fryer basket.
6. Air fry at 375°F (190°C) for 8-10 minutes, or until the egg rolls are golden brown and crispy.
7. Serve with a side of dipping sauce.

20. BBQ PULLED PORK TACOS

 Prep time: 10 minutes   **Servings:** 2

INGREDIENTS:

- 8 oz pulled pork (precooked)
- 4 small flour tortillas
- 1/2 cup coleslaw
- 2 tablespoons barbecue sauce

NUTRITIONAL INFO (PER SERVING):

Cal: 450 | Carbs: 35g | Pro: 24g
Fat: 23g | Sugars: 12g | Fiber: 3g

INSTRUCTIONS:

1. Place the precooked pulled pork in the air fryer basket.
2. Air fry at 375°F (190°C) for 8-10 minutes, or until the pork is heated through.
3. Warm the flour tortillas in the air fryer for 2 minutes.
4. Assemble the tacos by placing the pulled pork on the tortillas, topping with coleslaw, and drizzling with barbecue sauce.
5. Serve with a side of your choice.

SIDE DISHES

1. GARLIC PARMESAN FRIES

 Prep time: 10 minutes   **Servings:** 2

INGREDIENTS:

- 2 large russet potatoes, cut into fries
- 2 tablespoons olive oil
- 2 cloves garlic, minced
- 1/4 cup grated Parmesan cheese
- Salt and pepper to taste

NUTRITIONAL INFO (PER SERVING):

Cal: 324 | Carbs: 43g | Pro: 6g
Fat: 15g | Sugars: 1g | Fiber: 5g

INSTRUCTIONS:

1. Preheat your air fryer to 380°F (190°C).
2. In a large bowl, toss the potato fries with olive oil and minced garlic until evenly coated.
3. Place the seasoned fries in the air fryer basket, ensuring they are in a single layer.
4. Air fry for 15-20 minutes, shaking the basket every 5 minutes for even cooking, or until the fries are golden and crispy.
5. Remove the fries from the air fryer and immediately sprinkle with grated Parmesan cheese, salt, and pepper.
6. Serve hot.

2. AIR FRYER ONION RINGS

 Prep time: 15 minutes   **Servings:** 2

INGREDIENTS:

- 1 large onion, cut into 1/2-inch rings
- 1 cup all-purpose flour
- 2 eggs, beaten
- 1 cup bread crumbs
- Salt and pepper to taste

NUTRITIONAL INFO (PER SERVING):

Cal: 327 | Carbs: 63g | Pro: 10g
Fat: 4g | Sugars: 6g | Fiber: 4g

INSTRUCTIONS:

1. Preheat your air fryer to 375°F (190°C).
2. Dredge each onion ring in flour, then dip it in the beaten eggs, and finally coat it with bread crumbs.
3. Place the coated onion rings in the air fryer basket, ensuring they are in a single layer.
4. Air fry for 10-12 minutes, flipping the rings halfway through, or until they are golden brown and crispy.
5. Season with salt and pepper, and serve hot.

3. SWEET POTATO FRIES

 Prep time: 10 minutes   **Servings:** 2

INGREDIENTS:

- 2 medium sweet potatoes, cut into fries
- 2 tablespoons olive oil
- 1 teaspoon paprika
- Salt and pepper to taste

NUTRITIONAL INFO (PER SERVING):

Cal: 237 | Carbs: 33g | Pro: 3g
Fat: 11g | Sugars: 7g | Fiber: 5g

INSTRUCTIONS:

1. Preheat your air fryer to 375°F (190°C).
2. In a bowl, toss the sweet potato fries with olive oil and paprika until evenly coated.
3. Place the seasoned sweet potato fries in the air fryer basket, ensuring they are in a single layer.
4. Air fry for 15-18 minutes, shaking the basket every 5 minutes for even cooking, or until the fries are crispy and lightly browned.
5. Season with salt and pepper, and serve hot.

4. PARMESAN ROASTED ASPARAGUS

 Prep time: 10 minutes   **Servings:** 2

INGREDIENTS:

- 1 bunch asparagus spears, trimmed
- 2 tablespoons olive oil
- 1/4 cup grated Parmesan cheese
- Salt and pepper to taste

NUTRITIONAL INFO (PER SERVING):

Cal: 143 | Carbs: 4g | Pro: 7g
Fat: 12g | Sugars: 1g | Fiber: 2g

INSTRUCTIONS:

1. Preheat your air fryer to 375°F (190°C).
2. Toss the asparagus with olive oil in a bowl, ensuring they are coated evenly.
3. Place the asparagus in the air fryer basket.
4. Air fry for 6-8 minutes, or until the asparagus is tender and slightly crispy.
5. Sprinkle the roasted asparagus with grated Parmesan cheese, salt, and pepper.
6. Serve hot.

5. CRISPY BRUSSELS SPROUTS

 Prep time: 10 minutes   **Servings:** 2

INGREDIENTS:

- 1/2 lb Brussels sprouts, trimmed and halved
- 2 tablespoons olive oil
- 2 tablespoons balsamic vinegar
- Salt and pepper to taste

NUTRITIONAL INFO (PER SERVING):

Cal: 105 | Carbs: 8g | Pro: 3g
Fat: 7g | Sugars: 2g | Fiber: 3g

INSTRUCTIONS:

1. Preheat your air fryer to 375°F (190°C).
2. In a bowl, toss the Brussels sprouts with olive oil and balsamic vinegar.
3. Place the seasoned Brussels sprouts in the air fryer basket.
4. Air fry for 15-18 minutes, shaking the basket every 5 minutes for even cooking, or until the sprouts are crispy and caramelized.
5. Season with salt and pepper, and serve hot.

6. ZUCCHINI FRITTERS

 Prep time: 15 minutes   **Servings:** 2

INGREDIENTS:

- 2 medium zucchinis, grated
- 1/4 cup grated Parmesan cheese
- 1/4 cup breadcrumbs
- 1 egg
- Salt and pepper to taste

NUTRITIONAL INFO (PER SERVING):

Cal: 107 | Carbs: 12g | Pro: 8g
Fat: 4g | Sugars: 3g | Fiber: 2g

INSTRUCTIONS:

1. Grate the zucchinis and squeeze out excess moisture using a clean kitchen towel.
2. In a bowl, combine the grated zucchini, Parmesan cheese, breadcrumbs, egg, salt, and pepper. Mix well.
3. Form the mixture into patties and place them in the air fryer basket.
4. Air fry for 10-12 minutes, flipping the fritters halfway through, or until they are golden and crispy.
5. Serve hot.

7. ROASTED RED POTATOES

 Prep time: 10 minutes   **Servings:** 2

INGREDIENTS:

- 1 lb small red potatoes, halved
- 2 tablespoons olive oil
- 1 teaspoon dried rosemary
- Salt and pepper to taste

NUTRITIONAL INFO (PER SERVING):

Cal: 218 | Carbs: 33g | Pro: 4g
Fat: 9g | Sugars: 2g | Fiber: 3g

INSTRUCTIONS:

1. Preheat your air fryer to 375°F (190°C).
2. In a bowl, toss the red potato halves with olive oil and dried rosemary until coated evenly.
3. Place the seasoned potatoes in the air fryer basket.
4. Air fry for 18-20 minutes, shaking the basket every 5 minutes for even cooking, or until the potatoes are crispy and fork-tender.
5. Season with salt and pepper, and serve hot.

8. LOADED TATER TOTS

 Prep time: 15 minutes   **Servings:** 2

INGREDIENTS:

- 16 frozen tater tots
- 1/2 cup shredded cheddar cheese
- 2 slices bacon, cooked and crumbled
- 2 tablespoons sour cream
- Chopped chives for garnish (optional)

NUTRITIONAL INFO (PER SERVING):

Cal: 319 | Carbs: 23g | Pro: 9g
Fat: 21g | Sugars: 0g | Fiber: 2g

INSTRUCTIONS:

1. Preheat your air fryer to 400°F (200°C).
2. Arrange the frozen tater tots in a single layer in the air fryer basket.
3. Air fry for 15-18 minutes, shaking the basket every 5 minutes, or until the tots are golden and crispy.
4. Remove the tater tots from the air fryer and sprinkle with shredded cheddar cheese.
5. Return them to the air fryer for 1-2 minutes, or until the cheese is melted.
6. Top the tater tots with crumbled bacon, sour cream, and chopped chives.
7. Serve hot.

9. STUFFED MUSHROOMS

 Prep time: 15 minutes   **Servings:** 2

INGREDIENTS:

- 8 large mushrooms, stems removed and chopped
- 1/4 cup cream cheese
- 2 tablespoons grated Parmesan cheese
- 2 cloves garlic, minced
- Salt and pepper to taste

NUTRITIONAL INFO (PER SERVING):

Cal: 107 | Carbs: 3g | Pro: 5g
Fat: 8g | Sugars: 1g | Fiber: 1g

INSTRUCTIONS:

1. Preheat your air fryer to 350°F (175°C).
2. In a bowl, mix the chopped mushroom stems, cream cheese, grated Parmesan, minced garlic, salt, and pepper.
3. Stuff the mushroom caps with the cream cheese mixture.
4. Place the stuffed mushrooms in the air fryer basket.
5. Air fry for 10-12 minutes, or until the mushrooms are tender and the filling is golden.
6. Serve hot.

10. SPINACH AND ARTICHOKE DIP

 Prep time: 15 minutes   **Servings:** 2

INGREDIENTS:

- 1 cup frozen chopped spinach, thawed and drained
- 1 cup canned artichoke hearts, chopped
- 1/2 cup mayonnaise
- 1/2 cup grated Parmesan cheese
- Salt and pepper to taste

NUTRITIONAL INFO (PER SERVING):

Cal: 441 | Carbs: 11g | Pro: 5g
Fat: 42g | Sugars: 2g | Fiber: 4g

INSTRUCTIONS:

1. In a bowl, combine the chopped spinach, chopped artichoke hearts, mayonnaise, grated Parmesan, salt, and pepper.
2. Transfer the mixture to an oven-safe dish that fits in your air fryer basket.
3. Preheat your air fryer to 350°F (175°C).
4. Place the dish with the dip in the air fryer basket.
5. Air fry for 10-12 minutes, or until the dip is hot and bubbly.
6. Serve with tortilla chips or vegetable sticks.

11. BUFFALO CAULIFLOWER BITES

 Prep time: 15 minutes   **Servings:** 2

INGREDIENTS:

- 1/2 head cauliflower, cut into florets
- 1/2 cup buffalo sauce
- 2 tablespoons melted butter
- 1/4 cup blue cheese dressing
- Chopped chives for garnish

NUTRITIONAL INFO (PER SERVING):

Cal: 278 | Carbs: 6g | Pro: 4g Fat: 27g | Sugars: 2g | Fiber: 3g

INSTRUCTIONS:

1. Preheat your air fryer to 375°F (190°C).
2. In a bowl, combine the cauliflower florets, buffalo sauce, and melted butter.
3. Toss until the cauliflower is well coated.
4. Place the coated cauliflower in the air fryer basket.
5. Air fry for 12-15 minutes, shaking the basket every 5 minutes, or until the cauliflower is tender and crispy.
6. Serve with blue cheese dressing and garnish with chopped chives if desired.

12. CAPRESE SALAD SKEWERS

 Prep time: 10 minutes   **Servings:** 2

INGREDIENTS:

- 12 cherry tomatoes
- 12 fresh mozzarella balls
- 12 fresh basil leaves
- 2 tablespoons balsamic glaze
- Salt and pepper to taste

NUTRITIONAL INFO (PER SERVING):

Cal: 127 | Carbs: 5g | Pro: 7g Fat: 9g | Sugars: 3g | Fiber: 1g

INSTRUCTIONS:

1. Assemble the skewers by threading one cherry tomato, one mozzarella ball, and one basil leaf onto each skewer.
2. Arrange the skewers in the air fryer basket.
3. Preheat your air fryer to 350°F (175°C).
4. Air fry for 3-4 minutes, or until the mozzarella begins to melt.
5. Drizzle with balsamic glaze and season with salt and pepper.
6. Serve immediately.

13. GARLIC BREADSTICKS

 Prep time: 10 minutes   **Servings:** 2

INGREDIENTS:

- 4 slices of baguette or Italian bread
- 2 tablespoons butter, melted
- 2 cloves garlic, minced
- 2 tablespoons chopped fresh parsley
- Salt and pepper to taste

NUTRITIONAL INFO (PER SERVING):

Cal: 220 | Carbs: 26g | Pro: 4g
Fat: 12g | Sugars: 2g | Fiber: 2g

INSTRUCTIONS:

1. Preheat your air fryer to 350°F (175°C).
2. In a bowl, mix the melted butter, minced garlic, chopped fresh parsley, salt, and pepper.
3. Brush the garlic butter mixture over each slice of bread.
4. Place the bread slices in the air fryer basket.
5. Air fry for 4-5 minutes, or until the bread is toasted and slightly crispy.
6. Serve hot.

14. CRISPY EGGPLANT FRIES

 Prep time: 15 minutes   **Servings:** 2

INGREDIENTS:

- 1 medium eggplant, cut into fry-shaped sticks
- 1/2 cup breadcrumbs
- 1/4 cup grated Parmesan cheese
- Marinara sauce for dipping
- Salt and pepper to taste

NUTRITIONAL INFO (PER SERVING):

Cal: 185 | Carbs: 37g | Pro: 9g
Fat: 3g | Sugars: 7g | Fiber: 11g

INSTRUCTIONS:

1. Preheat your air fryer to 375°F (190°C).
2. In a bowl, combine the breadcrumbs, grated Parmesan, salt, and pepper.
3. Dredge each eggplant stick in the breadcrumb mixture, pressing to adhere.
4. Place the coated eggplant sticks in the air fryer basket.
5. Air fry for 10-12 minutes, shaking the basket every 5 minutes, or until the eggplant is crispy and golden.
6. Serve with marinara sauce for dipping.

15. AIR FRIED MOZZARELLA STICKS

 Prep time: 15 minutes　　 **Servings:** 2

INGREDIENTS:

- 6 mozzarella sticks, frozen
- 1/2 cup all-purpose flour
- 1 egg, beaten
- 1 cup breadcrumbs
- Marinara sauce for dipping

NUTRITIONAL INFO (PER SERVING):

Cal: 285 | Carbs: 29g | Pro: 10g
Fat: 14g | Sugars: 1g | Fiber: 2g

INSTRUCTIONS:

1. Preheat your air fryer to 390°F (200°C).
2. Dredge each frozen mozzarella stick in flour, then dip it in the beaten egg, and finally coat it with breadcrumbs.
3. Place the coated mozzarella sticks in the air fryer basket.
4. Air fry for 6-8 minutes, or until the mozzarella sticks are crispy and the cheese is melted.
5. Serve with marinara sauce for dipping.

16. STUFFED BELL PEPPERS

 Prep time: 20 minutes　　 **Servings:** 2

INGREDIENTS:

- 2 bell peppers, halved and seeded
- 1/2 cup cooked ground beef or turkey
- 1/2 cup cooked white rice
- 1/2 cup tomato sauce
- Salt and pepper to taste

NUTRITIONAL INFO (PER SERVING):

Cal: 223 | Carbs: 25g | Pro: 11g
Fat: 7g | Sugars: 6g | Fiber: 4g

INSTRUCTIONS:

1. Preheat your air fryer to 350°F (175°C).
2. In a bowl, mix the cooked ground meat, cooked white rice, tomato sauce, salt, and pepper.
3. Stuff each bell pepper half with the mixture.
4. Place the stuffed bell pepper halves in the air fryer basket.
5. Air fry for 15-18 minutes, or until the peppers are tender.
6. Serve hot.

17. AVOCADO FRIES WITH CHIPOTLE DIPPING SAUCE

 Prep time: 15 minutes   **Servings:** 2

INGREDIENTS:

- 2 avocados, sliced into wedges
- 1/2 cup breadcrumbs
- 1/4 cup grated Parmesan cheese
- 1 egg, beaten
- 2 tablespoons mayonnaise
- 1 tablespoon chipotle sauce
- Salt and pepper to taste

INSTRUCTIONS:

1. Preheat your air fryer to 375°F (190°C).
2. Dredge each avocado wedge in the beaten egg, then coat it with the breadcrumb mixture (breadcrumbs, grated Parmesan, salt, and pepper).
3. Place the coated avocado wedges in the air fryer basket.
4. Air fry for 8-10 minutes, shaking the basket every 5 minutes, or until the avocado fries are crispy and golden.
5. In a small bowl, mix the mayonnaise and chipotle sauce for the dipping sauce.
6. Serve the avocado fries with the chipotle dipping sauce.

NUTRITIONAL INFO (PER SERVING):

Cal: 409 | Carbs: 30g | Pro: 10g | Fat: 29g | Sugars: 2g | Fiber: 11g

18. FRIED PICKLES

 Prep time: 15 minutes   **Servings:** 2

INGREDIENTS:

- 1 cup dill pickle slices
- 1/2 cup all-purpose flour
- 1 egg, beaten
- 1/2 cup breadcrumbs
- Ranch dressing for dipping
- Salt and pepper to taste

INSTRUCTIONS:

1. Preheat your air fryer to 375°F (190°C).
2. Dredge each pickle slice in flour, then dip it in the beaten egg, and finally coat it with breadcrumbs.
3. Place the coated pickle slices in the air fryer basket.
4. Air fry for 6-8 minutes, or until the pickle slices are crispy and golden.
5. Serve with ranch dressing for dipping.

NUTRITIONAL INFO (PER SERVING):

Cal: 271 | Carbs: 45g | Pro: 8g
Fat: 7g | Sugars: 2g | Fiber: 3g

19. POTATO SKINS WITH BACON AND CHEESE

 Prep time: 20 minutes   **Servings:** 2

INGREDIENTS:

- 2 large russet potatoes
- 4 strips bacon, cooked and crumbled
- 1/2 cup shredded cheddar cheese
- 2 tablespoons sour cream
- Salt and pepper to taste

NUTRITIONAL INFO (PER SERVING):

Cal: 427 | Carbs: 41g | Pro: 13g
Fat: 24g | Sugars: 2g | Fiber: 4g

INSTRUCTIONS:

1. Preheat your air fryer to 375°F (190°C).
2. Wash and scrub the potatoes, then prick them with a fork in several places.
3. Air fry the whole potatoes for 40-45 minutes, or until they are tender and the skin is crispy.
4. Cut the potatoes in half lengthwise and scoop out the flesh, leaving a thin layer of potato.
5. Brush the potato skins with olive oil, then air fry them for an additional 5 minutes.
6. Fill each potato skin with shredded cheddar cheese and crumbled bacon.
7. Return the stuffed potato skins to the air fryer for 2-3 minutes, or until the cheese is melted and bubbly.
8. Top with sour cream, salt, and pepper, and serve hot.

20. TATER TOT NACHOS

 Prep time: 15 minutes   **Servings:** 2

INGREDIENTS:

- 2 cups frozen tater tots
- 1/2 cup shredded cheddar
- 1/2 cup cooked ground beef
- 2 tablespoons diced tomatoes
- 2 tablespoons diced green onions

NUTRITIONAL INFO (PER SERVING):

Cal: 431 | Carbs: 28g | Pro: 20g
Fat: 28g | Sugars: 2g | Fiber: 2g

INSTRUCTIONS:

1. Preheat your air fryer to 400°F (200°C).
2. Arrange the frozen tater tots in a single layer in the air fryer basket.
3. Air fry for 12-15 minutes, shaking the basket every 5 minutes, or until the tots are golden and crispy.
4. Sprinkle the tater tots with shredded cheddar cheese and cooked ground beef.
5. Return them to the air fryer for 1-2 minutes, or until the cheese is melted.
6. Top with diced tomatoes and green onions.
7. Serve hot.

VEGETABLES AND GRAINS

1. ROASTED VEGETABLES

 Prep time: 10 minutes   **Servings:** 2

INGREDIENTS:

- 2 cups of mixed vegetables (e.g., bell peppers, zucchini, carrots)
- 2 tablespoons of olive oil
- Salt and pepper to taste

NUTRITIONAL INFO (PER SERVING):

Cal: 120 | Carbs: 10g | Pro: 2g
Fat: 9g | Sugars: 4g | Fiber: 3g

INSTRUCTIONS:

1. Preheat your air fryer to 375°F (190°C).
2. Cut the mixed vegetables into bite-sized pieces.
3. Place the vegetables in a bowl and drizzle with olive oil. Season with salt and pepper, then toss to coat evenly.
4. Place the seasoned vegetables in the air fryer basket in a single layer.
5. Air fry for 12-15 minutes, shaking the basket halfway through, until the vegetables are roasted and tender.
6. Serve hot.

2. QUINOA STUFFED BELL PEPPERS

 Prep time: 15 minutes   **Servings:** 2

INGREDIENTS:

- 2 bell peppers, halved and seeds removed
- 1 cup cooked quinoa
- 1 cup black beans, drained and rinsed
- 1 cup salsa
- 1/2 cup shredded cheddar cheese

NUTRITIONAL INFO (PER SERVING):

Cal: 350 | Carbs: 57g | Pro: 15g
Fat: 7g | Sugars: 7g | Fiber: 12g

INSTRUCTIONS:

1. Preheat your air fryer to 350°F (175°C).
2. In a bowl, mix cooked quinoa, black beans, and salsa.
3. Stuff the bell pepper halves with the quinoa mixture.
4. Place the stuffed peppers in the air fryer basket.
5. Air fry for 15-20 minutes or until the peppers are tender.
6. Sprinkle shredded cheddar cheese on top and air fry for an additional 2 minutes or until the cheese is melted.
7. Serve hot.

3. MEDITERRANEAN VEGGIE WRAP

 Prep time: 10 minutes   **Servings:** 2

INGREDIENTS:

- 2 large tortillas
- 1 cup hummus
- 1 cup mixed greens
- 1/2 cup cherry tomatoes, halved
- 1/2 cup cucumber, thinly sliced

NUTRITIONAL INFO (PER SERVING):

Cal: 360 | Carbs: 43g | Pro: 11g
Fat: 16g | Sugars: 3g | Fiber: 8g

INSTRUCTIONS:

1. Lay out the tortillas and spread a generous amount of hummus on each one.
2. Evenly distribute mixed greens, cherry tomatoes, and cucumber on top of the hummus.
3. Roll up the tortillas tightly, folding in the sides as you go.
4. Slice in half diagonally, and your Mediterranean veggie wraps are ready to serve.

4. AIR FRYER FALAFEL

 Prep time: 15 minutes   **Servings:** 2

INGREDIENTS:

- 1 can (15 oz) chickpeas, drained and rinsed
- 1/4 cup chopped fresh parsley
- 1/4 cup chopped onion
- 1 teaspoon ground cumin
- 1/2 teaspoon salt

NUTRITIONAL INFO (PER SERVING):

Cal: 250 | Carbs: 45g | Pro: 13g
Fat: 4g | Sugars: 1g | Fiber: 13g

INSTRUCTIONS:

1. In a food processor, combine chickpeas, parsley, onion, cumin, and salt. Pulse until the mixture is coarsely ground but not pureed.
2. Form the mixture into small falafel patties.
3. Preheat your air fryer to 370°F (188°C).
4. Place the falafel patties in the air fryer basket in a single layer.
5. Air fry for 12-15 minutes, flipping the patties halfway through, until they are golden brown and crispy.
6. Serve the falafel with your favorite sauce or in pita bread.

5. PARMESAN ROASTED CAULIFLOWER

 Prep time: 10 minutes

 Servings: 2

INGREDIENTS:

- 1 small head of cauliflower, cut into florets
- 2 tablespoons of olive oil
- 1/2 cup grated Parmesan cheese
- Salt and pepper to taste

NUTRITIONAL INFO (PER SERVING):

Cal: 190 | Carbs: 10g | Pro: 10g
Fat: 14g | Sugars: 4g | Fiber: 4g

INSTRUCTIONS:

1. Preheat your air fryer to 375°F (190°C).
2. In a bowl, toss the cauliflower florets with olive oil, salt, and pepper.
3. Place the coated cauliflower in the air fryer basket.
4. Air fry for 15-18 minutes, shaking the basket halfway through, until the cauliflower is tender and golden brown.
5. Sprinkle grated Parmesan cheese over the cauliflower and air fry for an additional 2 minutes or until the cheese is melted and slightly crispy.
6. Serve hot.

6. BUTTERNUT SQUASH FRIES

 Prep time: 10 minutes

 Servings: 2

INGREDIENTS:

- 2 cups butternut squash, cut into thin fries
- 1 tablespoon olive oil
- 1 teaspoon paprika
- Salt and pepper to taste

NUTRITIONAL INFO (PER SERVING):

Cal: 110 | Carbs: 17g | Pro: 2g
Fat: 5g | Sugars: 2g | Fiber: 3g

INSTRUCTIONS:

1. Preheat your air fryer to 375°F (190°C).
2. In a bowl, toss the butternut squash fries with olive oil, paprika, salt, and pepper.
3. Place the seasoned fries in the air fryer basket in a single layer.
4. Air fry for 15-18 minutes, shaking the basket halfway through, until the fries are crispy and tender.
5. Serve hot as a side or snack.

7. CRISPY TOFU

 Prep time: 10 minutes   **Servings:** 2

INGREDIENTS:

- 8 oz extra-firm tofu, cubed
- 2 tablespoons soy sauce
- 1 tablespoon cornstarch
- 1 tablespoon sesame seeds (optional)
- Cooking spray

NUTRITIONAL INFO (PER SERVING):

Cal: 140 | Carbs: 8g | Pro: 11g
Fat: 8g | Sugars: 1g | Fiber: 1g

INSTRUCTIONS:

1. Preheat your air fryer to 375°F (190°C).
2. In a bowl, toss the tofu cubes with soy sauce and cornstarch until coated.
3. Sprinkle with sesame seeds if desired.
4. Lightly grease the air fryer basket with cooking spray.
5. Place the tofu in the basket in a single layer.
6. Air fry for 15-18 minutes, shaking the basket halfway through, until the tofu is crispy and golden.
7. Serve hot with your favorite dipping sauce.

8. STUFFED PORTOBELLO MUSHROOMS

 Prep time: 15 minutes   **Servings:** 2

INGREDIENTS:

- 2 large Portobello mushro-oms, stems removed
- 1 cup spinach
- 1/2 cup goat cheese
- 2 tablespoons balsamic glaze
- Salt and pepper to taste

NUTRITIONAL INFO (PER SERVING):

Cal: 180 | Carbs: 9g | Pro: 9g
Fat: 12g | Sugars: 4g | Fiber: 2g

INSTRUCTIONS:

1. Preheat your air fryer to 375°F (190°C).
2. In a pan, sauté the spinach until wilted. Season with salt and pepper.
3. Stuff the Portobello mushrooms with wilted spinach and goat cheese.
4. Place the stuffed mushrooms in the air fryer basket.
5. Air fry for 12-15 minutes, or until the mushrooms are tender and the cheese is slightly browned.
6. Drizzle balsamic glaze over the mushrooms and serve hot.

9. GREEK STYLE STUFFED PEPPERS

 Prep time: 15 minutes

 Servings: 2

INGREDIENTS:

- 2 bell peppers, halved and seeds removed
- 1 cup cooked rice
- 1/2 cup cooked ground lamb (or beef)
- 1/2 cup feta cheese
- 2 tablespoons chopped fresh parsley

INSTRUCTIONS:

1. Preheat your air fryer to 350°F (175°C).
2. In a bowl, mix cooked rice, cooked ground lamb, feta cheese, and chopped fresh parsley.
3. Stuff the bell pepper halves with the rice and lamb mixture.
4. Place the stuffed peppers in the air fryer basket.
5. Air fry for 15-20 minutes or until the peppers are tender and slightly browned.
6. Serve hot.

NUTRITIONAL INFO (PER SERVING):

Cal: 350 | Carbs: 34g | Pro: 16g Fat: 17g | Sugars: 4g | Fiber: 4g

10. AIR FRIED VEGGIE SPRING ROLLS

 Prep time: 15 minutes

 Servings: 2

INGREDIENTS:

- 4 spring roll wrappers
- 1 cup shredded cabbage
- 1/2 cup sliced bell peppers
- 1/2 cup shredded carrots
- 1/4 cup soy sauce for dipping

NUTRITIONAL INFO (PER SERVING):

Cal: 180 | Carbs: 36g | Pro: 4g
Fat: 1g | Sugars: 7g | Fiber: 3g

INSTRUCTIONS:

1. Lay out a spring roll wrapper and place a portion of shredded cabbage, sliced bell peppers, and shredded carrots in the center.
2. Fold the sides of the wrapper over the filling and then roll it up tightly, sealing the edge with a little water.
3. Repeat for the remaining wrappers and filling.
4. Preheat your air fryer to 375°F (190°C).
5. Lightly spray the spring rolls with cooking oil or use a pastry brush to apply a thin layer of oil.
6. Place the spring rolls in the air fryer basket.
7. Air fry for 10-12 minutes, turning them halfway through, until they are golden and crispy.
8. Serve hot with soy sauce for dipping.

11. GARLIC BUTTER MUSHROOMS

 Prep time: 10 minutes   **Servings:** 2

INGREDIENTS:

- 8 oz mushrooms, cleaned and halved
- 2 tablespoons melted butter
- 2 cloves garlic, minced
- Salt and pepper to taste
- Chopped fresh parsley for garnish (optional)

INSTRUCTIONS:

1. Preheat your air fryer to 375°F (190°C).
2. In a bowl, toss the mushroom halves with melted butter, minced garlic, salt, and pepper.
3. Place the seasoned mushrooms in the air fryer basket.
4. Air fry for 10-12 minutes, shaking the basket halfway through, until the mushrooms are tender and slightly browned.
5. Garnish with chopped fresh parsley if desired.
6. Serve hot as a side or topping for steak or chicken.

NUTRITIONAL INFO (PER SERVING):

Cal: 100 | Carbs: 4g | Pro: 2g | Fat: 9g | Sugars: 2g | Fiber: 1g

12. AIR FRIED QUINOA PATTIES

 Prep time: 20 minutes   **Servings:** 2

INGREDIENTS:

- 1 cup cooked quinoa
- 1/4 cup grated Parmesan cheese
- 1/4 cup breadcrumbs
- 1 egg
- 1/2 teaspoon Italian seasoning

INSTRUCTIONS:

1. In a bowl, mix cooked quinoa, grated Parmesan cheese, breadcrumbs, egg, and Italian seasoning until well combined.
2. Form the mixture into small patties.
3. Preheat your air fryer to 375°F (190°C).
4. Place the quinoa patties in the air fryer basket.
5. Air fry for 12-15 minutes, flipping the patties halfway through, until they are golden and crispy.
6. Serve hot with your favorite dipping sauce.

NUTRITIONAL INFO (PER SERVING):

Cal: 220 | Carbs: 29g | Pro: 10g
Fat: 7g | Sugars: 2g | Fiber: 3g

13. SPINACH AND FETA STUFFED BELL PEPPERS

 Prep time: 20 minutes   **Servings:** 2

INGREDIENTS:

- 2 bell peppers, halved and seeds removed
- 1 cup cooked quinoa
- 1 cup fresh spinach, chopped
- 1/2 cup crumbled feta
- Salt and pepper to taste

NUTRITIONAL INFO (PER SERVING):

Cal: 330 | Carbs: 44g | Pro: 12g
Fat: 13g | Sugars: 6g | Fiber: 6g

INSTRUCTIONS:

1. Preheat your air fryer to 350°F (175°C).
2. In a bowl, mix cooked quinoa, chopped spinach, crumbled feta cheese, salt, and pepper.
3. Stuff the bell pepper halves with the quinoa mixture.
4. Place the stuffed peppers in the air fryer basket.
5. Air fry for 15-20 minutes or until the peppers are tender.
6. Serve hot.

14. SPICY ROASTED CHICKPEAS

 Prep time: 10 minutes   **Servings:** 2

INGREDIENTS:

- 1 can (15 oz) chickpeas, drained and rinsed
- 1 tablespoon olive oil
- 1 teaspoon paprika
- 1/2 teaspoon cayenne pepper (adjust to taste)
- Salt to taste

NUTRITIONAL INFO (PER SERVING):

Cal: 180 | Carbs: 29g | Pro: 8g
Fat: 5g | Sugars: 5g | Fiber: 8g

INSTRUCTIONS:

1. Preheat your air fryer to 375°F (190°C).
2. In a bowl, toss the chickpeas with olive oil, paprika, cayenne pepper, and salt.
3. Place the seasoned chickpeas in the air fryer basket.
4. Air fry for 12-15 minutes, shaking the basket halfway through, until the chickpeas are crispy and slightly browned.
5. Serve as a spicy and crunchy snack.

15. PANKO-CRUSTED EGGPLANT

 Prep time: 15 minutes   **Servings:** 2

INGREDIENTS:

- 1 small eggplant, sliced into rounds
- 1/2 cup panko breadcrumbs
- 1/4 cup grated Parmesan
- 1 egg
- Salt and pepper to taste

NUTRITIONAL INFO (PER SERVING):

Cal: 190 | Carbs: 24g | Pro: 10g
Fat: 6g | Sugars: 4g | Fiber: 9g

INSTRUCTIONS:

1. Preheat your air fryer to 375°F (190°C).
2. In a bowl, beat the egg and season with salt and pepper.
3. In another bowl, combine panko breadcrumbs and grated Parmesan cheese.
4. Dip eggplant slices into the beaten egg, allowing any excess to drip off, and then coat with the breadcrumb mixture.
5. Place the coated eggplant slices in the air fryer basket.
6. Air fry for 12-15 minutes, flipping the slices halfway through, until they are golden brown and crispy.
7. Serve hot with your favorite dipping sauce.

16. AIR FRYER STUFFED ACORN SQUASH

 Prep time: 20 minutes   **Servings:** 2

INGREDIENTS:

- 1 acorn squash, halved and seeds removed
- 1 cup cooked quinoa
- 1/2 cup dried cranberries
- 1/4 cup chopped pecans
- 2 tablespoons maple syrup

NUTRITIONAL INFO (PER SERVING):

Cal: 400 | Carbs: 80g | Pro: 7g
Fat: 10g | Sugars: 24g | Fiber: 10g

INSTRUCTIONS:

1. Preheat your air fryer to 375°F (190°C).
2. In a bowl, mix cooked quinoa, dried cranberries, chopped pecans, and maple syrup.
3. Stuff each acorn squash half with the quinoa mixture.
4. Place the stuffed squash halves in the air fryer basket.
5. Air fry for 20-25 minutes or until the squash is tender and the filling is heated through.
6. Serve hot.

17. CAJUN CORN ON THE COB

 Prep time: 10 minutes   **Servings:** 2

INGREDIENTS:

- 2 ears of corn, husked and cleaned
- 2 tablespoons butter, melted
- 1 tablespoon Cajun seasoning
- Salt and pepper to taste

INSTRUCTIONS:

1. Preheat your air fryer to 375°F (190°C).
2. Brush the ears of corn with melted butter.
3. Season with Cajun seasoning, salt, and pepper.
4. Place the corn in the air fryer basket.
5. Air fry for 10-12 minutes, turning the corn occasionally, until it's tender and slightly charred.
6. Serve hot.

NUTRITIONAL INFO (PER SERVING):

Cal: 210 | Carbs: 26g | Pro: 4g
Fat: 11g | Sugars: 6g | Fiber: 4g

18. SWEET POTATO GNOCCHI

 Prep time: 10 minutes   **Servings:** 2

INGREDIENTS:

- 1 cup sweet potato gnocchi
- 2 tablespoons olive oil
- 2 tablespoons grated Parmesan cheese
- Salt and pepper to taste

INSTRUCTIONS:

1. Preheat your air fryer to 375°F (190°C).
2. Toss the sweet potato gnocchi with olive oil, salt, and pepper in a bowl.
3. Place the coated gnocchi in the air fryer basket.
4. Air fry for 10-12 minutes, shaking the basket halfway through, until the gnocchi is crispy and slightly browned.
5. Sprinkle grated Parmesan cheese over the gnocchi and air fry for an additional 2 minutes or until the cheese is melted and slightly crispy.
6. Serve hot.

NUTRITIONAL INFO (PER SERVING):

Cal: 320 | Carbs: 50g | Pro: 6g
Fat: 10g | Sugars: 4g | Fiber: 4g

19. AIR FRIED POLENTA BITES

 Prep time: 15 minutes   **Servings:** 2

INGREDIENTS:

- 8 oz cooked polenta, sliced into bite-sized rounds
- 2 tablespoons olive oil
- 1 teaspoon Italian seasoning
- Salt and pepper to taste

NUTRITIONAL INFO (PER SERVING):

Cal: 250 | Carbs: 27g | Pro: 3g
Fat: 16g | Sugars: 0g | Fiber: 2g

INSTRUCTIONS:

1. Preheat your air fryer to 375°F (190°C).
2. In a bowl, toss the polenta rounds with olive oil, Italian seasoning, salt, and pepper.
3. Place the seasoned polenta rounds in the air fryer basket.
4. Air fry for 12-15 minutes, flipping the rounds halfway through, until they are crispy and slightly browned.
5. Serve hot as an appetizer or side dish.

20. HERB AND PARMESAN POLENTA

 Prep time: 10 minutes   **Servings:** 2

INGREDIENTS:

- 1 cup cooked polenta
- 2 tablespoons grated Parmesan cheese
- 1 tablespoon chopped fresh herbs (e.g., basil, parsley)
- Salt and pepper to taste

NUTRITIONAL INFO (PER SERVING):

Cal: 210 | Carbs: 33g | Pro: 5g
Fat: 7g | Sugars: 2g | Fiber: 2g

INSTRUCTIONS:

1. Preheat your air fryer to 375°F (190°C).
2. In a bowl, mix cooked polenta, grated Parmesan cheese, chopped fresh herbs, salt, and pepper.
3. Shape the polenta mixture into small rounds or squares.
4. Place the polenta shapes in the air fryer basket.
5. Air fry for 10-12 minutes, flipping the shapes halfway through, until they are heated through and slightly crispy.
6. Serve hot as a side dish or appetizer.

SNACKS AND APPETIZERS

1. AIR FRYER POPCORN

 Prep time: 5 minutes   **Servings:** 2

INGREDIENTS:

- 1/2 cup popcorn kernels
- 1 tablespoon olive oil
- Salt to taste

NUTRITIONAL INFO (PER SERVING):

Cal: 120 | Carbs: 25g | Pro: 3g
Fat: 2g | Sugars: 0g | Fiber: 4g

INSTRUCTIONS:

1. Preheat your air fryer to 400°F (200°C).
2. Place the popcorn kernels in a single layer in the air fryer basket.
3. Drizzle the olive oil over the kernels and sprinkle with salt.
4. Cook for 10-12 minutes, shaking the basket every few minutes until the popping slows down.
5. Carefully remove the popcorn and let it cool for a minute before serving.

2. CRISPY CHICKPEA SNACKS

 Prep time: 5 minutes   **Servings:** 2

INGREDIENTS:

- 1 can (15 oz) chickpeas, drained and rinsed
- 1 tablespoon olive oil
- 1 teaspoon paprika
- Salt to taste

NUTRITIONAL INFO (PER SERVING):

Cal: 180 | Carbs: 27g | Pro: 7g
Fat: 6g | Sugars: 5g | Fiber: 7g

INSTRUCTIONS:

1. Preheat your air fryer to 375°F (190°C).
2. In a bowl, toss the chickpeas with olive oil, paprika, and salt.
3. Place the seasoned chickpeas in the air fryer basket.
4. Air fry for 15-20 minutes, shaking the basket every 5 minutes, until they are crispy.
5. Let them cool for a few minutes before serving.

3. AIR FRIED PICKLES

 Prep time: 10 minutes   **Servings:** 2

INGREDIENTS:

- 1 cup dill pickle slices, drained
- 1/2 cup panko breadcrumbs
- 1/4 cup grated Parmesan cheese
- Cooking spray

NUTRITIONAL INFO (PER SERVING):

Cal: 150 | Carbs: 20g | Pro: 6g
Fat: 6g | Sugars: 2g | Fiber: 2g

INSTRUCTIONS:

1. Preheat your air fryer to 400°F (200°C).
2. In a bowl, combine panko breadcrumbs and Parmesan cheese.
3. Dip pickle slices in the breadcrumb mixture, pressing the crumbs to adhere.
4. Place the coated pickles in a single layer in the air fryer basket.
5. Lightly spray them with cooking spray.
6. Air fry for 6-8 minutes until they are golden and crispy.
7. Serve with your favorite dipping sauce.

4. BUFFALO CAULIFLOWER BITES

 Prep time: 10 minutes   **Servings:** 2

INGREDIENTS:

- 2 cups cauliflower florets
- 2 tablespoons buffalo sauce
- 1/4 cup panko breadcrumbs
- Cooking spray

NUTRITIONAL INFO (PER SERVING):

Cal: 90 | Carbs: 15g | Pro: 5g
Fat: 2g | Sugars: 2g | Fiber: 4g

INSTRUCTIONS:

1. Preheat your air fryer to 375°F (190°C).
2. In a bowl, toss cauliflower florets with buffalo sauce.
3. Dip each piece in panko breadcrumbs, pressing the crumbs to adhere.
4. Place the coated cauliflower in the air fryer basket.
5. Lightly spray them with cooking spray.
6. Air fry for 10-12 minutes until they are crispy and tender.
7. Serve with ranch or blue cheese dressing.

5. SWEET POTATO FRIES WITH DIPPING SAUCE

 Prep time: 10 minutes   **Servings:** 2

INGREDIENTS:

- 2 medium sweet potatoes, cut into fries
- 1 tablespoon olive oil
- Salt and pepper to taste
- 1/4 cup mayonnaise
- 1 tablespoon ketchup

NUTRITIONAL INFO (PER SERVING):

Cal: 250 | Carbs: 28g | Pro: 2g
Fat: 15g | Sugars: 8g | Fiber: 4g

INSTRUCTIONS:

1. Preheat your air fryer to 400°F (200°C).
2. In a bowl, toss sweet potato fries with olive oil, salt, and pepper.
3. Place the seasoned fries in the air fryer basket.
4. Air fry for 15-20 minutes, shaking the basket every 5 minutes until they are crispy and cooked through.
5. While the fries cook, mix mayonnaise and ketchup to create the dipping sauce.
6. Serve the sweet potato fries with the dipping sauce.

6. MOZZARELLA STUFFED MEATBALLS

 Prep time: 15 minutes   **Servings:** 2

INGREDIENTS:

- 4 frozen meatballs
- 4 mozzarella cheese cubes
- 1/2 cup marinara sauce
- 1 tablespoon grated Parmesan cheese

NUTRITIONAL INFO (PER SERVING):

Cal: 350 | Carbs: 10g | Pro: 25g
Fat: 22g | Sugars: 4g | Fiber: 2g

INSTRUCTIONS:

1. Preheat your air fryer to 375°F (190°C).
2. Make an indentation in each frozen meatball and insert a mozzarella cheese cube.
3. Place the stuffed meatballs in the air fryer basket.
4. Air fry for 12-15 minutes until they are cooked through and cheese is melted.
5. Heat marinara sauce and serve the meatballs with sauce and a sprinkle of grated Parmesan.

7. SPINACH AND ARTICHOKE DIP

 Prep time: 10 minutes   **Servings:** 2

INGREDIENTS:

- 1 cup frozen spinach, thawed and drained
- 1 cup canned artichoke hearts, drained and chopped
- 1/2 cup mayonnaise
- 1/4 cup grated Parmesan cheese

NUTRITIONAL INFO (PER SERVING):

Cal: 380 | Carbs: 11g | Pro: 5g
Fat: 35g | Sugars: 1g | Fiber: 3g

INSTRUCTIONS:

1. Preheat your air fryer to 350°F (175°C).
2. In a bowl, mix together spinach, artichoke hearts, mayonnaise, and grated Parmesan cheese.
3. Transfer the mixture to an oven-safe dish that fits in the air fryer.
4. Air fry for 10-12 minutes until the dip is heated through and bubbly.
5. Serve with tortilla chips or vegetable sticks.

8. AIR FRYER CALAMARI

 Prep time: 15 minutes   **Servings:** 2

INGREDIENTS:

- 1/2 lb calamari rings
- 1/2 cup all-purpose flour
- 1/2 teaspoon salt
- 1/4 teaspoon black pepper

NUTRITIONAL INFO (PER SERVING):

Cal: 220 | Carbs: 26g | Pro: 14g
Fat: 6g | Sugars: 1g | Fiber: 1g

INSTRUCTIONS:

1. Preheat your air fryer to 375°F (190°C).
2. In a bowl, combine flour, salt, and black pepper.
3. Dredge the calamari rings in the flour mixture.
4. Place the coated calamari in the air fryer basket.
5. Air fry for 8-10 minutes until they are golden and crispy.
6. Serve with marinara sauce or aioli.

9. STUFFED MUSHROOMS

 Prep time: 10 minutes **Servings:** 2

INGREDIENTS:

- 8 large white mushrooms, stems removed
- 1/4 cup cream cheese
- 1/4 cup grated Parmesan cheese
- Salt and pepper to taste

NUTRITIONAL INFO (PER SERVING):

Cal: 150 | Carbs: 5g | Pro: 6g
Fat: 11g | Sugars: 3g | Fiber: 1g

INSTRUCTIONS:

1. Preheat your air fryer to 350°F (175°C).
2. In a bowl, mix cream cheese, grated Parmesan cheese, salt, and pepper.
3. Stuff each mushroom cap with the cream cheese mixture.
4. Place the stuffed mushrooms in the air fryer basket.
5. Air fry for 8-10 minutes until they are cooked through and lightly browned.
6. Serve hot.

10. GARLIC BREADSTICKS

 Prep time: 10 minutes **Servings:** 2

INGREDIENTS:

- 4 frozen garlic breadsticks
- 2 tablespoons butter, melted
- 1/2 teaspoon garlic powder
- 1/2 teaspoon dried parsley

NUTRITIONAL INFO (PER SERVING):

Cal: 240 | Carbs: 27g | Pro: 4g
Fat: 14g | Sugars: 1g | Fiber: 2g

INSTRUCTIONS:

1. Preheat your air fryer to 350°F (175°C).
2. Brush the frozen garlic breadsticks with melted butter.
3. Sprinkle garlic powder and dried parsley over the breadsticks.
4. Place the breadsticks in the air fryer basket.
5. Air fry for 5-7 minutes until they are crispy and golden.
6. Serve with marinara sauce or as a side.

11. CRISPY EGGPLANT FRIES

 Prep time: 15 minutes   **Servings:** 2

INGREDIENTS:

- 1 small eggplant, cut into fries
- 1/2 cup panko breadcrumbs
- 1/4 cup grated Parmesan cheese
- Cooking spray

NUTRITIONAL INFO (PER SERVING):

Cal: 190 | Carbs: 29g | Pro: 8g
Fat: 6g | Sugars: 7g | Fiber: 6g

INSTRUCTIONS:

1. Preheat your air fryer to 375°F (190°C).
2. In a bowl, combine panko breadcrumbs and grated Parmesan cheese.
3. Dip eggplant fries in the breadcrumb mixture, pressing the crumbs to adhere.
4. Place the coated eggplant in the air fryer basket.
5. Lightly spray them with cooking spray.
6. Air fry for 10-12 minutes until they are crispy and tender.
7. Serve with marinara sauce.

12. POTATO SKINS WITH BACON AND CHEESE

 Prep time: 15 minutes   **Servings:** 2

INGREDIENTS:

- 2 large russet potatoes
- 2 strips of bacon, cooked and crumbled
- 1/2 cup shredded cheddar cheese
- Salt and pepper to taste

NUTRITIONAL INFO (PER SERVING):

Cal: 280 | Carbs: 33g | Pro: 12g
Fat: 11g | Sugars: 1g | Fiber: 4g

INSTRUCTIONS:

1. Preheat your air fryer to 400°F (200°C).
2. Scrub the potatoes and prick them with a fork.
3. Place the potatoes in the air fryer and cook for 35-40 minutes until they are tender.
4. Allow the potatoes to cool slightly, then cut them in half and scoop out the insides, leaving about 1/4 inch of flesh.
5. Sprinkle the potato skins with bacon and cheddar cheese.
6. Place the filled skins in the air fryer basket.
7. Air fry for 5-7 minutes until the cheese is melted and the skins are crispy.
8. Season with salt and pepper, and serve.

13. CAPRESE SALAD SKEWERS

 Prep time: 10 minutes   **Servings:** 2

INGREDIENTS:

- 8 cherry tomatoes
- 8 small fresh mozzarella balls
- 8 fresh basil leaves
- Balsamic glaze for drizzling

NUTRITIONAL INFO (PER SERVING):

Cal: 160 | Carbs: 4g | Pro: 12g
Fat: 10g | Sugars: 2g | Fiber: 1g

INSTRUCTIONS:

1. Thread a cherry tomato, a mozzarella ball, and a basil leaf onto each skewer.
2. Place the skewers in the air fryer basket.
3. Air fry for 3-5 minutes until the mozzarella begins to soften.
4. Drizzle with balsamic glaze before serving.

14. AIR FRIED MOZZARELLA STICKS

 Prep time: 10 minutes   **Servings:** 2

INGREDIENTS:

- 6 mozzarella string cheese sticks
- 1/2 cup panko breadcrumbs
- 1/4 cup marinara sauce
- Cooking spray

NUTRITIONAL INFO (PER SERVING):

Cal: 220 | Carbs: 19g | Pro: 14g
Fat: 9g | Sugars: 3g | Fiber: 1g

INSTRUCTIONS:

1. Preheat your air fryer to 375°F (190°C).
2. Cut each string cheese stick in half.
3. Dip each cheese piece in water, then coat with panko breadcrumbs.
4. Place the coated cheese sticks in the air fryer basket.
5. Lightly spray them with cooking spray.
6. Air fry for 5-7 minutes until they are golden and the cheese is melted.
7. Serve with marinara sauce.

15. LOADED SWEET POTATO NACHOS

 Prep time: 15 minutes   **Servings:** 2

INGREDIENTS:

- 2 medium sweet potatoes, sliced into rounds
- 1/2 cup shredded cheddar
- 1/4 cup cooked ground beef
- 1/4 cup diced tomatoes
- Salt and pepper to taste

NUTRITIONAL INFO (PER SERVING):

Cal: 300 | Carbs: 28g | Pro: 16g
Fat: 15g | Sugars: 7g | Fiber: 5g

INSTRUCTIONS:

1. Preheat your air fryer to 375°F (190°C).
2. Place the sweet potato rounds in the air fryer basket.
3. Air fry for 12-15 minutes until they are crispy and cooked through.
4. Sprinkle cheddar cheese over the sweet potato rounds.
5. Air fry for an additional 2-3 minutes until the cheese is melted.
6. Top with cooked ground beef, diced tomatoes, and season with salt and pepper.
7. Serve as nachos.

16. AIR FRIED MAC AND CHEESE BITES

 Prep time: 15 minutes   **Servings:** 2

INGREDIENTS:

- 1 cup cooked macaroni and cheese, chilled
- 1/2 cup panko breadcrumbs
- Cooking spray

NUTRITIONAL INFO (PER SERVING):

Cal: 230 | Carbs: 32g | Pro: 6g
Fat: 9g | Sugars: 3g | Fiber: 1g

INSTRUCTIONS:

1. Preheat your air fryer to 375°F (190°C).
2. Scoop small portions of chilled macaroni and cheese and shape them into bite-sized balls.
3. Roll each mac and cheese ball in panko breadcrumbs to coat.
4. Place the coated mac and cheese bites in the air fryer basket.
5. Lightly spray them with cooking spray.
6. Air fry for 5-7 minutes until they are golden and crispy.
7. Serve with your favorite dipping sauce.

17. AVOCADO FRIES WITH CHIPOTLE DIPPING SAUCE

 Prep time: 15 minutes   **Servings:** 2

INGREDIENTS:

- 1 ripe avocado, cut into fries
- 1/2 cup panko breadcrumbs
- 1/4 cup chipotle mayo
- Cooking spray

NUTRITIONAL INFO (PER SERVING):

Cal: 320 | Carbs: 21g | Pro: 3g
Fat: 25g | Sugars: 2g | Fiber: 7g

INSTRUCTIONS:

1. Preheat your air fryer to 375°F (190°C).
2. Dip avocado fries in panko breadcrumbs, pressing the crumbs to adhere.
3. Place the coated avocado fries in the air fryer basket.
4. Lightly spray them with cooking spray.
5. Air fry for 6-8 minutes until they are crispy and golden.
6. Serve with chipotle mayo for dipping.

18. TATER TOT NACHOS

 Prep time: 15 minutes   **Servings:** 2

INGREDIENTS:

- 2 cups frozen tater tots
- 1/2 cup shredded cheddar cheese
- 1/4 cup cooked ground beef
- 1/4 cup diced tomatoes
- Salt and pepper to taste

NUTRITIONAL INFO (PER SERVING):

Cal: 350 | Carbs: 28g | Pro: 16g
Fat: 20g | Sugars: 1g | Fiber: 3g

INSTRUCTIONS:

1. Preheat your air fryer to 400°F (200°C).
2. Place the frozen tater tots in the air fryer basket.
3. Air fry for 15-20 minutes until they are crispy and golden.
4. Sprinkle cheddar cheese over the tater tots.
5. Air fry for an additional 2-3 minutes until the cheese is melted.
6. Top with cooked ground beef, diced tomatoes, and season with salt and pepper.
7. Serve as nachos.

19. BBQ CHICKEN SLIDERS

 Prep time: 15 minutes   **Servings:** 2

INGREDIENTS:

- 2 small chicken breasts
- 1/4 cup BBQ sauce
- 2 small hamburger buns
- 1/4 cup coleslaw

NUTRITIONAL INFO (PER SERVING):

Cal: 450 | Carbs: 45g | Pro: 27g
Fat: 17g | Sugars: 18g
Fiber: 3g

INSTRUCTIONS:

1. Preheat your air fryer to 375°F (190°C).
2. Brush the chicken breasts with BBQ sauce.
3. Place the chicken in the air fryer basket.
4. Air fry for 15-20 minutes, flipping halfway, until the chicken is cooked through.
5. While the chicken cooks, lightly toast the buns in the air fryer for 2-3 minutes.
6. Assemble the sliders with chicken, coleslaw, and additional BBQ sauce.

20. BACON-WRAPPED JALAPEÑO POPPERS

 Prep time: 15 minutes   **Servings:** 2

INGREDIENTS:

- 4 fresh jalapeño peppers
- 4 tablespoons cream cheese
- 4 slices of bacon
- Toothpicks

NUTRITIONAL INFO (PER SERVING):

Cal: 230 | Carbs: 3g | Pro: 5g
Fat: 22g | Sugars: 1g | Fiber: 1g

INSTRUCTIONS:

1. Preheat your air fryer to 375°F (190°C).
2. Cut jalapeños in half lengthwise and remove the seeds and membranes.
3. Fill each jalapeño half with cream cheese.
4. Wrap each jalapeño half with a slice of bacon and secure with a toothpick.
5. Place the bacon-wrapped jalapeños in the air fryer basket.
6. Air fry for 10-12 minutes until the bacon is crispy and jalapeños are tender.
7. Serve as appetizers.

DESSERTS

1. AIR FRYER APPLE PIE EGG ROLLS

 Prep time: 15 minutes   **Servings:** 2

INGREDIENTS:

- 2 egg roll wrappers
- 1 cup apple pie filling
- 1/2 teaspoon cinnamon
- 1 tablespoon melted butter

NUTRITIONAL INFO (PER SERVING):

Cal: 250 | Carbs: 50g | Pro: 2g
Fat: 6g | Sugars: 26g | Fiber: 2g

INSTRUCTIONS:

1. Preheat your air fryer to 350°F (180°C).
2. Lay an egg roll wrapper on a clean surface.
3. Place 1/2 cup of apple pie filling in the center of the wrapper. Sprinkle with cinnamon.
4. Fold in the sides of the wrapper, then roll it up like a burrito, sealing the edges with a bit of water.
5. Brush the egg roll with melted butter.
6. Place the egg rolls in the air fryer basket in a single layer.
7. Air fry for 8-10 minutes, turning halfway, until golden brown and crisp.
8. Remove and let cool slightly before serving.

2. CINNAMON SUGAR DONUT HOLES

 Prep time: 10 minutes   **Servings:** 2

INGREDIENTS:

- 1 can refrigerated biscuit dough
- 1/4 cup granulated sugar
- 1 teaspoon ground cinnamon
- 2 tablespoons melted butter

NUTRITIONAL INFO (PER SERVING):

Cal: 280 | Carbs: 34g | Pro: 2g
Fat: 15g | Sugars: 12g | Fiber: 1g

INSTRUCTIONS:

1. Preheat your air fryer to 350°F (180°C).
2. Cut each biscuit into quarters.
3. In a bowl, combine sugar and cinnamon.
4. Dip each biscuit piece in melted butter, then roll in the cinnamon sugar mixture.
5. Place the coated dough pieces in the air fryer basket.
6. Air fry for 5-6 minutes until golden brown and cooked through.
7. Serve warm.

3. CHURRO BITES

 Prep time: 10 minutes   **Servings:** 2

INGREDIENTS:

- 1 can refrigerated crescent roll dough
- 1/4 cup granulated sugar
- 1 teaspoon ground cinnamon
- 2 tablespoons melted butter

NUTRITIONAL INFO (PER SERVING):

Cal: 350 | Carbs: 38g | Pro: 3g
Fat: 21g | Sugars: 20g | Fiber: 1g

INSTRUCTIONS:

1. Preheat your air fryer to 350°F (180°C).
2. Roll out the crescent roll dough and pinch the seams to seal.
3. Cut the dough into bite-sized pieces.
4. In a bowl, combine sugar and cinnamon.
5. Dip each dough piece in melted butter, then roll in the cinnamon sugar mixture.
6. Place the coated dough pieces in the air fryer basket.
7. Air fry for 6-8 minutes until golden brown.
8. Serve warm.

4. AIR FRIED BANANA SPLITS

 Prep time: 5 minutes   **Servings:** 2

INGREDIENTS:

- 2 bananas
- 4 scoops of vanilla ice cream
- 1/4 cup chocolate syrup
- 1/4 cup whipped cream

NUTRITIONAL INFO (PER SERVING):

Cal: 410 | Carbs: 64g | Pro: 4g
Fat: 16g | Sugars: 43g | Fiber: 5g

INSTRUCTIONS:

1. Preheat your air fryer to 350°F (180°C).
2. Slice each banana in half lengthwise.
3. Place the banana halves in the air fryer basket and air fry for 3-4 minutes until they caramelize.
4. Place two banana halves on each plate.
5. Top with two scoops of vanilla ice cream, drizzle with chocolate syrup, and add a dollop of whipped cream.
6. Serve immediately.

5. NUTELLA STUFFED CRESCENT ROLLS

 Prep time: 10 minutes   **Servings:** 2

INGREDIENTS:

- 1 can refrigerated crescent roll dough
- 2 tablespoons Nutella
- 1 tablespoon powdered sugar
- 1/2 teaspoon cocoa powder (for dusting)

NUTRITIONAL INFO (PER SERVING):

Cal: 280 | Carbs: 39g | Pro: 3g
Fat: 13g | Sugars: 16g | Fiber: 1g

INSTRUCTIONS:

1. Preheat your air fryer to 350°F (180°C).
2. Roll out the crescent roll dough and separate into triangles.
3. Place 1 tablespoon of Nutella on each triangle and spread it out.
4. Roll up the triangles, sealing the edges.
5. Place the stuffed rolls in the air fryer basket.
6. Air fry for 6-8 minutes until golden brown.
7. In a small bowl, mix powdered sugar and cocoa powder.
8. Dust the cooked crescent rolls with the sugar-cocoa mixture.
9. Serve warm.

6. MINI CHERRY HAND PIES

 Prep time: 15 minutes   **Servings:** 2

INGREDIENTS:

- 1 sheet of refrigerated pie dough
- 1/2 cup cherry pie filling
- 1 tablespoon milk
- 1/4 cup powdered sugar (for glaze)

NUTRITIONAL INFO (PER SERVING):

Cal: 280 | Carbs: 48g | Pro: 2g
Fat: 10g | Sugars: 26g
Fiber: 1g

INSTRUCTIONS:

1. Preheat your air fryer to 350°F (180°C).
2. Roll out the pie dough and cut it into 4 equal squares.
3. Place 2 tablespoons of cherry pie filling in the center of each square.
4. Fold the squares in half to create triangle-shaped pies.
5. Seal the edges with a fork.
6. Brush the tops with milk.
7. Place the hand pies in the air fryer basket.
8. Air fry for 8-10 minutes until golden brown.
9. In a small bowl, mix powdered sugar with a little water to make a glaze.
10. Drizzle the glaze over the hand pies.
11. Serve warm.

7. AIR FRYER S'MORES

 Prep time: 5 minutes   **Servings:** 2

INGREDIENTS:

- 4 graham crackers
- 2 large marshmallows
- 1/4 cup chocolate chips

NUTRITIONAL INFO (PER SERVING):

Cal: 180 | Carbs: 34g | Pro: 3g
Fat: 6g | Sugars: 19g | Fiber: 2g

INSTRUCTIONS:

1. Preheat your air fryer to 350°F (180°C).
2. Break the graham crackers in half to create 8 squares.
3. Place 4 squares on the bottom of the air fryer basket.
4. Top each square with chocolate chips and a marshmallow.
5. Place the remaining graham cracker squares on top to make sandwiches.
6. Air fry for 2-3 minutes, until the marshmallows are toasted and chocolate is melted.
7. Serve immediately.

8. FRIED OREOS

 Prep time: 10 minutes   **Servings:** 2

INGREDIENTS:

- 8 Oreo cookies
- 1/2 cup pancake mix
- 1/4 cup milk
- Vegetable oil (for frying)

NUTRITIONAL INFO (PER SERVING):

Cal: 320 | Carbs: 62g | Pro: 4g
Fat: 6g | Sugars: 34g | Fiber: 1g

INSTRUCTIONS:

1. Preheat your air fryer to 350°F (180°C).
2. In a bowl, mix the pancake mix and milk to create a batter.
3. Dip each Oreo in the batter, ensuring it's fully coated.
4. Place the coated Oreos in the air fryer basket.
5. Air fry for 3-4 minutes until they are golden and crispy.
6. Remove and let them cool slightly before serving.

9. AIR FRIED BROWNIE BITES

 Prep time: 10 minutes   **Servings:** 2

INGREDIENTS:

- 1/2 cup brownie mix
- 2 tablespoons vegetable oil
- 2 tablespoons water

NUTRITIONAL INFO (PER SERVING):

Cal: 350 | Carbs: 51g | Pro: 3g
Fat: 16g | Sugars: 31g | Fiber: 2g

INSTRUCTIONS:

1. Preheat your air fryer to 350°F (180°C).
2. In a bowl, mix brownie mix, vegetable oil, and water until smooth.
3. Drop small spoonfuls of the batter onto the air fryer basket.
4. Air fry for 6-8 minutes until the brownie bites are firm on the outside and slightly gooey inside.
5. Let them cool for a few minutes before serving

10. APPLE CRISP

 Prep time: 10 minutes   **Servings:** 2

INGREDIENTS:

- 2 cups apple slices
- 1/4 cup rolled oats
- 2 tablespoons brown sugar
- 2 tablespoons melted butter

NUTRITIONAL INFO (PER SERVING):

Cal: 280 | Carbs: 49g | Pro: 2g
Fat: 10g | Sugars: 32g | Fiber: 6g

INSTRUCTIONS:

1. Preheat your air fryer to 350°F (180°C).
2. In a bowl, mix apple slices with 1 tablespoon of melted butter.
3. In another bowl, combine rolled oats, brown sugar, and the remaining melted butter.
4. Layer the apple slices in the air fryer basket and top with the oat mixture.
5. Air fry for 8-10 minutes until the topping is crispy and the apples are tender.
6. Serve warm.

11. PEACH COBBLER

 Prep time: 10 minutes   **Servings:** 2

INGREDIENTS:

- 1 cup canned peaches in syrup
- 1/2 cup biscuit mix
- 1/4 cup milk
- 2 tablespoons melted butter

NUTRITIONAL INFO (PER SERVING):

Cal: 370 | Carbs: 57g | Pro: 3g
Fat: 15g | Sugars: 31g | Fiber: 1g

INSTRUCTIONS:

1. Preheat your air fryer to 350°F (180°C).
2. In a bowl, mix the biscuit mix and milk until a dough forms.
3. In an oven-safe dish that fits in your air fryer, pour the canned peaches and their syrup.
4. Drop spoonfuls of the biscuit dough over the peaches.
5. Drizzle with melted butter.
6. Place the dish in the air fryer basket.
7. Air fry for 10-12 minutes until the topping is golden and the filling is bubbling.
8. Serve warm.

12. AIR FRYER BEIGNETS

 Prep time: 15 minutes   **Servings:** 2

INGREDIENTS:

- 1 can refrigerated biscuit dough
- 1/4 cup powdered sugar
- 1/2 teaspoon ground cinnamon (optional)
- Vegetable oil (for frying)

NUTRITIONAL INFO (PER SERVING):

Cal: 280 | Carbs: 46g | Pro: 2g
Fat: 10g | Sugars: 19g | Fiber: 1g

INSTRUCTIONS:

1. Preheat your air fryer to 350°F (180°C).
2. In a bowl, mix powdered sugar and ground cinnamon (if using) and set it aside.
3. Cut each biscuit into quarters.
4. Drop the biscuit pieces into the air fryer basket in a single layer.
5. Air fry for 5-6 minutes until golden brown.
6. Remove and immediately toss them in the powdered sugar mixture.
7. Serve warm.

13. AIR FRIED CINNAMON ROLLS

 Prep time: 10 minutes   **Servings:** 2

INGREDIENTS:

- 4 cinnamon rolls (from a can)
- 1/4 cup cream cheese frosting
- 1/4 teaspoon ground cinnamon (optional)

NUTRITIONAL INFO (PER SERVING):

Cal: 400 | Carbs: 52g | Pro: 4g
Fat: 20g | Sugars: 29g | Fiber: 1g

INSTRUCTIONS:

1. Preheat your air fryer to 350°F (180°C).
2. Place the cinnamon rolls in the air fryer basket.
3. Air fry for 6-8 minutes until they're golden brown and cooked through.
4. Drizzle with cream cheese frosting.
5. Sprinkle with ground cinnamon if desired.
6. Serve warm.

14. AIR FRYER FUNNEL CAKES

 Prep time: 10 minutes   **Servings:** 2

INGREDIENTS:

- 1 cup pancake mix
- 1/2 cup water
- 1/4 cup powdered sugar
- Vegetable oil (for frying)

NUTRITIONAL INFO (PER SERVING):

Cal: 320 | Carbs: 61g | Pro: 4g
Fat: 6g | Sugars: 26g | Fiber: 1g

INSTRUCTIONS:

1. Preheat your air fryer to 350°F (180°C).
2. In a bowl, mix pancake mix and water until you have a smooth batter.
3. Transfer the batter to a squeeze bottle or a plastic bag with a small hole cut in the corner.
4. Drizzle the batter into the air fryer in a circular pattern to create a funnel cake shape.
5. Air fry for 4-6 minutes until golden and crispy.
6. Remove and dust with powdered sugar.
7. Serve immediately.

15. MINI CHEESECAKES

 Prep time: 10 minutes

 Servings: 2

INGREDIENTS:

- 2 graham cracker crusts
- 1/2 cup cream cheese
- 1/4 cup granulated sugar
- 1 egg

NUTRITIONAL INFO (PER SERVING):

Cal: 420 | Carbs: 38g | Pro: 6g
Fat: 29g | Sugars: 26g | Fiber: 1g

INSTRUCTIONS:

1. Preheat your air fryer to 350°F (180°C).
2. In a bowl, beat cream cheese, sugar, and egg until well combined.
3. Pour the cream cheese mixture into the graham cracker crusts.
4. Place the cheesecakes in the air fryer basket.
5. Air fry for 10-12 minutes until set and slightly golden on top.
6. Let them cool and refrigerate for at least 1 hour before serving.

16. AIR FRIED STRAWBERRY SHORTCAKE

 Prep time: 10 minutes

 Servings: 2

INGREDIENTS:

- 2 shortcakes
- 1 cup fresh strawberries, sliced
- 1/2 cup whipped cream
- 2 tablespoons powdered sugar

NUTRITIONAL INFO (PER SERVING):

Cal: 330 | Carbs: 54g | Pro: 3g
Fat: 10g | Sugars: 33g | Fiber: 3g

INSTRUCTIONS:

1. Preheat your air fryer to 350°F (180°C).
2. Split the shortcakes in half.
3. Place the bottom halves in the air fryer basket.
4. Air fry for 2-3 minutes until they're slightly crispy.
5. Top with sliced strawberries and a dollop of whipped cream.
6. Place the top halves on and dust with powdered sugar.
7. Serve immediately.

17. CHOCOLATE LAVA CAKES

 Prep time: 15 minutes   **Servings:** 2

INGREDIENTS:

- 2/3 cup chocolate chips
- 1/4 cup butter
- 2 eggs
- 2 tablespoons sugar
- 2 tablespoons all-purpose flour

NUTRITIONAL INFO (PER SERVING):

Cal: 600 | Carbs: 50g | Pro: 7g
Fat: 43g | Sugars: 36g
Fiber: 3g

INSTRUCTIONS:

1. Preheat your air fryer to 375°F (190°C).
2. In a microwave-safe bowl, melt the chocolate chips and butter in 30-second increments, stirring until smooth.
3. In another bowl, beat eggs, sugar, and flour until well combined.
4. Pour the melted chocolate mixture into the egg mixture and stir until smooth.
5. Grease two ramekins or small oven-safe dishes.
6. Divide the batter between the dishes.
7. Place the dishes in the air fryer basket.
8. Air fry for 8-10 minutes until the edges are set but the centers are still slightly gooey.
9. Let them cool for a few minutes before serving.

18. BLUEBERRY HAND PIES

 Prep time: 15 minutes   **Servings:** 2

INGREDIENTS:

- 1 sheet refrigerated pie dough
- 1/2 cup blueberry pie filling
- 1 tablespoon milk
- 1/4 cup powdered sugar (for glaze)

NUTRITIONAL INFO (PER SERVING):

Cal: 320 | Carbs: 51g | Pro: 3g
Fat: 12g | Sugars: 24g
Fiber: 1g

INSTRUCTIONS:

1. Preheat your air fryer to 350°F (180°C).
2. Roll out the pie dough and cut it into 4 equal squares.
3. Place 2 tablespoons of blueberry pie filling in the center of each square.
4. Fold the squares in half to create triangle-shaped pies.
5. Seal the edges with a fork.
6. Brush the tops with milk.
7. Place the hand pies in the air fryer basket.
8. Air fry for 8-10 minutes until golden brown.
9. In a small bowl, mix powdered sugar with a little water to make a glaze.
10. Drizzle the glaze over the hand pies.
11. Serve warm.

19. PUMPKIN SPICE DONUT HOLES

 Prep time: 15 minutes   **Servings:** 2

INGREDIENTS:

- 1 can refrigerated biscuit dough
- 1/4 cup powdered sugar
- 1/2 teaspoon pumpkin spice
- 2 tablespoons melted butter

NUTRITIONAL INFO (PER SERVING):

Cal: 330 | Carbs: 43g | Pro: 2g
Fat: 16g | Sugars: 22g | Fiber: 1g

INSTRUCTIONS:

1. Preheat your air fryer to 350°F (180°C).
2. Roll out the biscuit dough and cut it into small pieces.
3. Roll the pieces into small balls.
4. Place the dough balls in the air fryer basket.
5. Air fry for 6-8 minutes until golden brown and cooked through.
6. In a bowl, mix powdered sugar and pumpkin spice.
7. Toss the cooked dough balls in the sugar-spice mixture.
8. Drizzle with melted butter.
9. Serve warm.

20. AIR FRYER RICE KRISPIE TREATS

 Prep time: 15 minutes   **Servings:** 2

INGREDIENTS:

- 2 cups Rice Krispies cereal
- 1/4 cup butter
- 2 cups mini marshmallows

NUTRITIONAL INFO (PER SERVING):

Cal: 320 | Carbs: 63g | Pro: 2g
Fat: 8g | Sugars: 29g | Fiber: 0g

INSTRUCTIONS:

1. Preheat your air fryer to 350°F (180°C).
2. In a microwave-safe bowl, melt the butter and marshmallows in 30-second increments, stirring until smooth.
3. Add the Rice Krispies cereal and mix until well combined.
4. Line a small dish or pan with parchment paper and press the mixture into it.
5. Place the dish or pan in the air fryer basket.
6. Air fry for 3-4 minutes until the top is lightly toasted.
7. Let it cool and then cut into squares before serving.

BONUS

Thank You for Exploring the Culinary Delights of the
"5 Ingredients Air Fryer Cookbook" by Violet Harmond!

YOUR FEEDBACK MATTERS!

Dear Valued Reader,
Thank you for embarking on this delicious journey with the *"5 Ingredients Air Fryer Cookbook"*.
We hope you've enjoyed the recipes and found inspiration in the simplicity and flavor-packed
wonders of air fryer cooking.

Your Review Matters: If this cookbook has added a dash of culinary joy to your life, we kindly ask you to consider leaving a
review on Amazon. Your thoughts and experiences can guide future readers in making an informed decision.
Your review is not just feedback; it's a beacon for those seeking a delightful culinary adventure.
Your support is immensely appreciated!

HOW TO LEAVE A REVIEW:

- Go to the book's Amazon page.
- Scroll down to the "Customer Reviews" section.
- Click on "Write a Customer Review."
- Remember, your words can make a world of difference!

EXCLUSIVE BONUS CONTENT AWAITS!

As a token of our gratitude, we're excited to offer you an exclusive bonus.
Simply scan the QR code below with your smartphone,
and you'll receive a special bonus directly to your email address.

HOW TO CLAIM YOUR BONUS:

- Open your smartphone camera.
- Align it with the QR code.
- Once scanned, follow the instructions on your screen to claim your bonus.

Thank you once again for being a part of the *"5 Ingredients Air Fryer Cookbook"* community.
We hope these recipes continue to bring joy and flavor to your kitchen.

Happy Cooking!

Warm Regards,
Violet Harmond.

Printed in Great Britain
by Amazon